IN STEP
WITH
GOD

UNDERSTANDING HIS WAYS
AND PLANS FOR YOUR LIFE

CHARLES F. STANLEY

THOMAS NELSON
Since 1798

NASHVILLE DALLAS MEXICO CITY RIO DE JANEIRO

Published in Nashville, Tennessee, by Thomas Nelson. Thomas Nelson is a registered trademark of Thomas Nelson, Inc.

Thomas Nelson, Inc., titles may be purchased in bulk for educational, business, fund-raising, or sales promotional use. For information, please e-mail SpecialMarkets@ThomasNelson.com.

Unless otherwise noted, Scripture quotations are from the NEW AMERICAN STANDARD BIBLE®, © The Lockman Foundation 1960, 1962, 1963, 1968, 1971, 1972, 1973, 1975, 1977, 1995. Used by permission.

Scripture quotations noted NIV are from the HOLY BIBLE: NEW INTERNATIONAL VERSION®. © 1973, 1978, 1984 by International Bible Society. Used by permission of Zondervan Publishing House. All rights reserved.

ISBN 978-1-4002-0288-1 (trade paper)

Library of Congress Cataloging-in-Publication Data

Stanley, Charles F.
In step with God : understanding His ways and plans for your life / Charles F. Stanley.
p. cm.
ISBN 978-1-4002-0091-7
1. Spirituality I. Title.
BV4501.3.S7333 2008
248.4—dc22   2008029598

Printed in the United States of America

10 11 12 13 14 RRD 5 4 3 2 1

*This book is dedicated to my special friend Sid,
who beautifully illustrates a life in step with God.*

Let me know Your ways that I may know You,
so that I may find favor in Your sight.

—Exodus 33:13

CONTENTS

INTRODUCTION

Some years ago, I remember watching my grandson as he tried to operate a toy he had been given. His hands moved quickly—passing over every detail of the object as he searched for the right turn or switch that would bring the object to life. No matter how hard he tried, nothing worked. I reached across the table where we were sitting and picked up the instructions. The first step told us where to place the batteries and alerted us to the fact that they needed to be positioned in a certain direction. I double-checked what we had done earlier and found that one was positioned incorrectly. Grateful for the set of instructions, I made the change and continued reading. Step two told us where the on/off switch was located. And step three encouraged us to be sure that the item was placed firmly on the floor because if we had done what we were supposed to do, there would be action. A second later, that was exactly what happened—lots of action and lots of fun.

Many other times I was very glad that I had a set of instructions to help me understand what I needed to do. Mostly these were times when I wanted to understand God's ways *not* just so I could make a good decision, though that is extremely important, but so I could know Him—the way He operates, thinks—and know His intimate love for me. Moses prayed, "If I have found favor in Your sight, let me *know Your ways* that I may know You, so that I may find favor in Your sight" (Ex. 33:13, *emphasis added*). This became my prayer and my greatest desire.

In reading this passage, I noticed that Moses used the phrase "favor in Your sight" twice in one sentence. It is obvious he had one clear goal, and that was to know God. He was not satisfied with knowing a little something about Him. He wanted to understand the way He worked so he could know Him better. I believe Moses understood that this could be a reality. The Lord had spoken to him at the burning bush, but He also had made His presence known on many other occasions. He revealed His power and ability to save at the crossing of the Red Sea. Yet these two events did not tell Israel's deliverer what he wanted to know. He wanted to know God on an intimate level—something much deeper than just realizing He exists. His quest to know the Lord led him to a deeper level—one that changed his life focus forever.

Would you like to know God and also know that you are walking in step with His will and plan for your life? If you are a believer, your answer is more than likely yes. But you may not be sure how to do this. You read your Bible, go to church, and give your tithe, but you know very little about His nature and His characteristics. You know He loves you, yet you have not experienced the depth of His love intimately and personally. Until you begin to understand His ways, a spiritual shade will remain closed in your life. You may know right from wrong in certain areas, but do you have knowledge of why God wants you to live a certain way? What motivates Him? Why does He do what He does? Why does He respond the way He responds? Why does He act the way He acts? Once you begin to understand the way God thinks and operates, you will understand Him better, and suddenly you will realize that your knowledge of God has deepened and your desire to please Him has increased. A light goes on inside your heart and mind, and you realize that He loves you with an eternal love.

Over the years, I have listened as people expressed their desire to understand how God works. Many have said, "If only I knew what He wanted me to do, I would do it." Others have tried desperately to make sense out of tragic or challenging circumstances only to come away feeling more alone. Often this happens because they are not truly seeking to know the Lord but are simply looking for relief from their emotional and mental stress and pain. God will reveal Himself to us. But before He does, we must come to a point where we surrender to Him. This means that we desire to know Him more than we desire to have our way. The men and women used by God have hearts solely devoted to Him.

Moses drew near to the Lord, and we must decide to do the same. To refuse is to miss the awesome opportunity of knowing the infinite God of the universe. The secret to knowing Him is not found any other place than in an intimate and loving relationship with the Savior. Moses saw the burning bush, and he was drawn to it. Within his heart was a growing passion to know the one true God.

Likewise, Joshua encountered the angel of the Lord hours before Israel was scheduled to march on the city of Jericho. He had heard Moses tell of the first time he stood in God's presence. Therefore, at the Lord's command, he immediately removed his shoes as an outward sign of humble adoration to God. Similarly, after hearing the angel's words spoken to her, Mary replied, "Behold, the bondslave of the Lord; may it be done to me according to your word" (Luke 1:38). Neither of these people or countless others whose lives intersected with the Lord were solely interested in their personal comfort and care. Each one came to a point where his greater hunger and thirst were to know God. *Show me, and teach me Your ways that I may know You* was the cry of their hearts. With deep emotion, David wrote, "As the deer pants for the water brooks, so my soul pants for You, O God. My soul thirsts for God, for the living God" (Ps. 42:1–2).

These words represented David's passionate pursuit to know and understand God's ways so that he might become the person whom God called "a man after My heart" (Acts 13:22). David's enemies were in a red-hot quest to hunt him down, but fear would not conquer his heart. He wanted God to know that his deepest longing was to know Him. From the depths of despair he wrote,

> Deep calls to deep at the sound of Your waterfalls;
> All Your breakers and Your waves have rolled over me.
> The LORD will command His lovingkindness in the daytime;
> And His song will be with me in the night. (Ps. 42:7–8)

The more we learn about God, the more our lives change. We learn to rest in the fact that He is God, and He is at work. We may not know all there is to know about His ways, but we learn quickly that He is sovereign, in control, and willing to guide us at every turn. What security this brings to our hearts and minds.

Getting to know God may include walking with Him through life's darkest valleys. But in these times we gain tremendous wisdom into the heart and mind of God. Some of the greatest lessons I have learned have come as the result of inexpressible heartache. Could God have spared me from disappointment? Yes, but that was not His will, His way, or His plan for my life. He had greater things He wanted to teach me, and they could be learned only through sorrow and suffering. I never encourage anyone to pray for trouble. But when it does strike, I counsel people to be still and ask Him to show them what they need to learn through the situation. The prophet Jeremiah tells us to draw near to God and He will reveal "great and mighty things" to our hearts and minds (Jer. 33:3).

Far too many people have a surface knowledge of God. They know something about Him, but they do not know Him. They wonder, *Where is God? What is He like? Can I know Him personally? Does He care about me?* The answer: yes! He is here, right now, right beside you. He has never moved, and He never will. He is your loving heavenly Father who wants to make Himself available to you. Just as He called to Moses, He calls to you—asking you to draw near and learn His ways so that you may know and experience the great depths of His love and care.

This is my prayer for everyone who reads this book: that you would pray what Moses prayed, "Let me know Your ways that I may know You, so that I may find favor in Your sight" (Ex. 33:13). When you begin to understand God's mind and the way He works, you suddenly have the right tools to live an abundant life—one that is full and complete. And beyond this, you also will have the greatest Source of knowledge, love, peace, joy, intimacy, and hope abiding within you. Nothing is more valuable than knowing God. The world may entice you to search for wisdom in any number of ways, but there is only one Source of truth, and He is waiting to reveal Himself to you.

Chapter One

INTIMACY WITH GOD: AN ESSENTIAL REQUIREMENT

If you were to ask me to tell you about my mother, I would begin by telling you that her name was Rebecca and she was born in Dry Fork, Virginia. After her parents died, she helped raise her family. She did not have much education, but she was committed to doing the best she could. I also might add that she passed away a number of years ago. With this small amount of information, you would not know very much about my mother.

However, what if I told you that she was pretty and a very godly woman who always provided for me? My father died when I was quite young, and she willingly accepted the challenge of raising me. At one point, she worked two jobs in order to pay our bills and keep food on our table. Most of the time, she got up extremely early to go to work. While I was in school, she came home from her first job and prepared to go to her second job. Before she left, she would cook dinner and set the table for me so I would know exactly what to do and what to eat. She would lay it all out, and without fail, she would write me a note telling me things that I needed to remember or sometimes she would just write, "Charles, I love you."

Mom was disciplined and persistent. She had to be in order to keep our family together. She never gave up and never quit. Even though life was difficult, she rarely became discouraged. She always wanted me to look my best. Therefore, at night she washed and ironed my overalls so I would have a fresh pair for school the next morning. I had only two pairs. She would make sure that my shoes were shined and that I had a handkerchief in my pocket. Anytime I went to her with a problem, she never said, "Charles, I'm too busy to talk." She always stopped whatever she was doing and listened. Sometimes I did not make very good grades, but Mom never scolded me. She would say, "Do the best you can, and I will pray for you." Almost every night, she would come into my bedroom and kneel beside my bed. Then we would pray together. I can still recall how she said my name to the Lord while praying about the things that concerned me. I saw her become angry only a couple of times. She was far more forgiving than I knew how to be.

Even though she made just nine dollars and ten cents a week, we got through the difficult times. I can remember her sitting down, going over the bills, and saying, "This needs to go to this bill and this much on this one," and so on. She was meticulous and careful with money. Yet she also was very giving. There were times when we had little to eat. However, if someone dropped by who had less than we did, Mom always found something in the refrigerator to give to him or her. There are many things I remember about her, but the one thing that I will never forget is how much she sacrificed for me. If I stopped at this point and asked, "Do you know something about my mother?" I believe you would say yes.

Relationship Counts

If I asked you to tell me about God, what would you say? Could you tell me about the personal relationship you have with Him? Or would you say, "There is only one of Him. He lives in heaven, and I believe that His Son died for my sins. He has promised to create a place for me in heaven. He saved me, justified me, and forgave me"? I probably could list a few more doctrinal truths, but the real questions are: Do you know who God is? Do you know something personal about Him that goes beyond what you have learned while sitting in church or having conversations with a friend? Do you know His ways? Far too many people do not understand the way He works. The problem is, many of God's people know *about* Him, but they do not have a personal relationship *with* Him. And this is where we face our greatest challenge—knowing God and loving Him above all else. The bottom line to any relationship is this: if you want to know someone, you must know him or her intimately.

Over the years, the word *intimacy* has been redefined and misinterpreted by our morally out-of-step society. Having intimacy within a relationship does not mean having sexual contact. True intimacy is involved in fellowship with others. You can have a friendship and not be intimate with that person. You can become intimately involved in his or her life, but this does not mean that you are involved in a sexual relationship. Two friends can enjoy knowing each other on a very deep level. In fact, having close friends—intimates—is very reflective of God's nature because this is exactly what He desires from you and me—a close, personal, and especially intimate relationship. Many people are satisfied with just knowing a few things about God but not knowing Him deeply. True, unbridled intimacy touches the soul and the hidden places of our hearts like nothing else can. It goes much deeper than physical expression. And only God has the ability to love us intimately and unconditionally. He created us for one purpose, and that is to have fellowship with Him.

He wants you to know that He loves you. And there is nothing you can do to surprise or disappoint Him because He knows all things and is never shocked by your actions. Although He does not approve of sin, He loves the sinner. Therefore, when you do sin, you have an Advocate before the Father— Jesus Christ—who hears when you pray for forgiveness and cares when you are hurting. God may discipline you when you yield to temptation, but He will never withhold His love from you. This truth never changes. It never shifts and never fades. He is righteous and steadfast: "For the LORD your God is a merciful God; he will not abandon or destroy you" (Deut. 4:31 NIV). You are His workmanship—created in His image for good works (Eph. 2:10). There is within the heart of every man and woman a place that only God can fill. You may try to satisfy your longings with different things. But until you come to a point of full surrender to Him, you remain vulnerable to fearful thoughts, feelings of discontentment, selfish desires, as well as pride and lust. Fellowship with God starts at the very core of your being. It shifts your focus from being me-centered to Christ-centered. When you develop an intimate relationship with the heavenly Father, you discover He is surrounding you with His eternal care. Abraham drew near to the Lord, and as a result of his desire to know Him, he learned the ways of God. He did not resist God's instruction, and he proved to be faithful. The Lord granted him extreme wisdom and knowledge because he had learned the secret to tapping into the heart of God.

You cannot do His will unless you learn to walk in His ways. Think about the human relationships you have. As long as you hold someone at arm's length, you cannot know him or her. However, the moment you open up and begin talking to the other person, you start to develop a relationship. If you keep your emotional walls up, then the other person will sense this. Over time, he or she will find a way to break through or break away. Friendships—abiding relationships—can exist and grow only through mutual intimacy.

Prayer Is Essential

Where do we begin our step-by-step walk with God? Jesus taught His disciples to pray (Luke 11:1–4). Therefore, you must begin with prayer. One man told me, "I don't want to get into anything too deep in prayer. I'm not a very emotional person. I enjoy church, but I'm not one of those people who does a lot of talking to God. I mean, what would I say to Him? He knows everything anyway." One of the greatest desires of God's heart is that you and I would desire to know Him—not just give lip service to Him on Sundays but truly long to know Him and His ways. He wants to build an intimate relationship with us, but do we desire the same thing when it comes to Him? Do we want to know Him? To achieve this, we must also learn His ways. We may do this by drawing near to God, as James wrote: "Draw near to God and He will draw near to you" (James 4:8).

The intimate moments we share with the Savior are the very times when He reveals Himself to us. With our minds focused on loving and worshiping Him, we sense His closeness. Moses wanted to know God. His quest was not simply to gain a type of human knowledge. He wanted to know Him as a Friend and a personal, holy God. God wanted to show Moses how to live in the light of His favor and blessing: "Whenever Moses entered the tent, the pillar of cloud would descend and stand at the entrance of the tent; and the Lord would speak with Moses. When all the people saw the pillar of cloud standing at the entrance of the tent, all the people would arise and worship, each at the entrance of his tent. Thus the Lord used to speak to Moses face to face, just as a man speaks to his *friend*" (Ex. 33:9–11, *emphasis added*). The word *friend* in this context means "intimate companion." God never intended for us to know only about Him. He wants us to come to know Him—His ways and His unconditional love for us.

Many times, the British people scoff at Americans, saying we are often quick to engage in conversation but fall short when it comes to building deep relationships. On the other hand, they may appear standoffish when first introduced; however, once they have formed a close friendship, it usually lasts a lifetime. The closer in fellowship we become with God, the more we will trust Him. This is true for every relationship. The more time we spend with a friend, the more we learn about him or her, and the more we rely on that person. As trust increases, we find ourselves opening up and talking about the feelings we have and challenges we face. Trust and intimacy are tightly woven together. If we do not sense we can trust a person, we probably won't take time to get to know him or her. And even if we do, we will be cautious.

A Heart for God

The nearer I draw to the Lord, the more I will know about Him—His love for me and His good plans and desires for my life. Plus, the more intimate I become with God, the better I understand His ways, and this understanding leads to a deeper longing to know God better. I learn how to discern His will not only for my life but also for the situations I encounter. Many times, we run up against challenges that threaten to destroy our peace and security. If we have developed a close relationship with the Savior, we can be still and trust Him to show us how to respond. He also will give us insight into the motivations of others. Without realizing it, we may end up in a situation that may not be God's best. While God's desire is to provide the wisdom and insight we need to make good decisions, we must be in a position to accept His guidance. Although Moses did not perfectly understand God's ways, he still wanted to know Him. One of the most honest experiences we can have comes when we realize that we can be ourselves before the Lord and know that He loves and accepts us. The disciples made the choice to come to Jesus. He made Himself available to them, but they had to choose to come. Those who heard the Savior speak chose to listen and draw near. Their lives changed so dramatically that many left all they had in order to follow Him.

Moses was not just curious about God; he was intently interested and made his way up the mountain to a place where he witnessed the fiery evidence of God's presence burning before him. The Bible tells us, "The angel of the LORD appeared to him in a blazing fire from the midst of a bush; and he looked, and behold, the bush was burning with fire, yet the bush was not consumed. . . . When the LORD *saw* that he turned aside to look, God called to him from the midst of the bush and said, 'Moses, Moses!' And he said, 'Here I am'" (Ex. 3:2, 4, *emphasis added*). God Himself spoke to Moses. Anytime there is a reference to the angel of the Lord, we know that is Christ and that God is with us. Another thing we need to understand is that God chose something like an insignificant bush on the back side of a mountain as His staging point for the deliverance of His people. If He had wanted to, He could have set the entire mountainside on fire, but He didn't. He wanted to see whether Moses would respond and whether his heart was truly broken and ready to be used. God knew the answer because He is omniscient, but He wanted Moses to know as well. He knows exactly what we will do, even before an event or certain circumstance arises. Yet He had a goal in mind for positioning Moses in a place where he could see the bush that was not consumed by fire.

The time Moses spent before the burning bush was crucial to everything else that followed. Had he not turned aside to see God's presence, he would have missed the most awesome opportunity ever given. That was the point where his personal relationship with God began. It was the place where he began to discover there was much more to knowing God than anything he had heard. The relationship that grew between him and the Lord spanned decades that included times of heartache, joy, sorrow, celebration, frustration, friendship, and deep, abiding love. More important, these moments spent in the presence of God signaled the beginning of Moses' journey into deeper wisdom and an intimate knowledge of God and His ways. Once we begin to understand God's ways, we gain a clearer understanding of life. And we develop an intense desire to know Him.

By the end of this book, I believe your view of God will change. Your love for Him will grow deeper as you allow Him to teach you about who He is and not just who someone says He is. Remember what Jesus asked His disciples?

He asked, "Who do people say that I am?" (Mark 8:27). He knew exactly who He was, but He wanted to hear what His disciples would say—those who had been with Him and were His most intimate and trusted friends. They fumbled for an answer and then told Him, "John the Baptist; and others say Elijah; but others, one of the prophets" (v. 28).

In Christ's day there were many religious misconceptions. A common one was called *Elijah redivivus*, which taught that the prophet Elijah had come back from the dead. Obviously some people who followed the Savior wondered if these misleading theories could be true. However, these false teachings were not what actually troubled the Lord. He was focused on the fact that He had been with the disciples for nearly three years, and it appeared that they still did not understand who He was. He was their Lord and Savior and friend. Did they truly know this? He wanted His closest companions to realize that He was the Son of God. Therefore, He became even more direct with His questioning: "But who do you say that I am?" Peter could not resist the urge to speak and answered, "You are the Christ" (v. 29), or *Christos*, which means "Messiah—the Anointed One." Jesus came to earth not only to save us from our sins but also to provide a way for us to know the heavenly Father. He was God in the flesh, and yet He was their teacher, master, and friend. Today, through the presence and power of the Holy Spirit, we have the opportunity to know God personally and intimately. Many times, we fail to realize the importance of knowing Him. Yet when trials come or heartaches become too much for us, we cry out, longing for His sovereign and omnipotent touch.

Understanding What You Believe

In reading the Scriptures, we may wonder, *How did the apostle Paul experience severe suffering without abandoning his faith?* There was only one way, and that was through faith and intimate fellowship with God. How did David not only survive but also thrive during years of being pursued by King Saul—a man who had lost his focus and had become fixated on David's destruction? There was only one way: he maintained a focus on the Lord. The intimate relationship he built with God when he was a young shepherd boy carried over to his adult years. The time he had spent tending his father's flock was not useless or wasted. It provided the right setting and atmosphere for him to know the Lord. Later after he was grown and adversity, misunderstanding, and disappointment came his way, he recalled all the times he had been in God's presence. He also recalled the faithfulness of the Lord. When you, as David did, understand the power that is yours in Christ, fear loses its effectiveness. You realize that whatever comes your way passes through the loving hands of the Savior first. People who refuse to accept this truth from God's Word often find this hard to understand. But David understood it perfectly, and in Psalm 18, he wrote,

> The LORD is my rock and my fortress and my deliverer,
> My God, my rock, in whom I take refuge;
> My shield and the horn of my salvation, my stronghold.
> I call upon the LORD, who is worthy to be praised,
> And I am saved from my enemies. (vv. 2–3)

If I gave you a sheet of paper, could you fill it up with the many ways that God works in your life? What about a four-by-six card or a three-by-five card? Or would you tell me that your knowledge of Him is so small that you could fit it on a postage stamp? Through trial and difficulty—heartache and deep sorrow—men and women like David, Moses, and many others learned the ways of God. Confronted with the awesomeness of God's presence, Mary, who became the Lord's mother, prayed: "My soul glorifies the Lord and my spirit rejoices in God my Savior, for he has been mindful of the humble state of his servant" (Luke 1:46-48 NIV). They found that His love never changes and that He is completely trustworthy. In Psalm 25, David proclaimed,

> To You, O LORD, I lift up my soul.
> O my God, in You I trust,
> Do not let me be ashamed;
> Do not let my enemies exult over me.
> Indeed, none of those who wait for You will be ashamed;
> Those who deal treacherously without cause will be ashamed.
> Make me know Your ways, O LORD;
> Teach me Your paths.
> Lead me in Your truth and teach me,
> For You are the God of my salvation;
> For You I wait all the day. (vv. 1–5)

God's love, power, strength, and abiding care are anchors to our hearts and souls in times of great distress. If we are intimately involved with Him, then when the storms of life hit and the winds of adversity blow hard against us, we can quickly discern how to stand firm in our faith. We also will be able to spot Satan's lies, which are words always framed in fear, destruction, and personal ruin. You do not have to fall prey to his attack. By learning His ways, you will have all you need to stand firm in your faith at every turn in life. God also will equip you so that you can grow in your knowledge of Him.

One young woman said that on the night she was saved, she prayed, "Lord, teach me more about You. Place me in a church where I can learn about Your ways." He will not resist this heartfelt attitude, and I pray this is the prayer of your heart—that you will want to know Him, His ways, His personal care, and His will for your life.

Chapter Two

GOD'S WAY IS THE BEST WAY

The psalmist wrote that God "made known His ways to Moses" (Ps. 103:7). The omniscient, omnipresent, omnipotent God of the universe revealed Himself to a man—someone who was very much like you and me. Moses had passion and strong desires. He was tenacious and bold. But like us, he also made mistakes. When he saw God's people being mistreated, he wanted to do something to change their circumstances—and he did not want to wait. This proved to be a wrong decision.

Years ago, we had a staff vacancy at First Baptist Atlanta that needed to be filled. The position had been open for several months, and though we had interviewed a list of people, no one seemed right. Finally a friend who was also a pastor called me and passed along the name of a man who he felt would be a perfect fit. I arranged a meeting with the man, but later, after we had talked, I was not convinced that he was the one. In fact, I sensed God's Spirit warning me not to move forward by hiring him. My staff was swayed in the opposite direction. Everyone seemed to feel that he was perfect. I was amazed by their acceptance of him. So, I reconsidered my first impression. *When I met him, was I having a bad day? Was there something personal about him that I did not like?* When I prayed about it, I could not come up with a reason not to hire him. I just had this deep, inner rustling that I believed was from God, cautioning me not to do it.

After several more weeks, the pressure to hire someone for the position became very great, and I gave in to the requests of others. I hired this person but had to dismiss him a year later. More than likely, you have gone through a similar situation. You may have been asked to take part in a particular event or function, and deep inside you could sense God saying, *Don't do it. It is not My best.* God could have acted in a major way to stop me from hiring this person. But instead, He allowed me to go through this time of indecision, which ended up with me making the wrong choice, in order to teach me more about His ways.

His ways include not only His actions and deeds but also how He thinks and what motivates Him. Usually when we are in the middle of learning more about Him, we have to ignore the advice of others. This is not always the case, but many opportunities He places before us require being alone with Him in concentrated prayer. To do this, we need to set aside time to seek His will. Yet there is another aspect to being alone with God, and it is this: we can be in a packed room with others while maintaining a central focus of peace and willingness to obey God.

Moses spent years in the desert learning how to live a solitary life. There were others around him, but not the throngs of people that he was accustomed to knowing in Egypt. Until we learn how to abide with Christ, our lives will be marked by moments of poorly orchestrated decisions. In this situation, I knew what was correct, but I allowed myself to be swayed by others who were convinced they knew what was best. Don't ever compromise your convictions. Even if you are the last person standing, remain steadfast to what God has given you to do because His way is the best way.

He rarely, if ever, lays out His entire plan before asking you to move forward trusting Him. In this particular situation, we had interviewed a lot of people, and the temptation to "get the position filled" cost us greatly. Though I'm sure Moses had many natural traits, patience was probably not one of his stronger points. However, the two that won God's favor were Moses' desire to draw near to the burning bush and later his obedience to the Lord's will. God watches to see what we will do when we face a challenge, receive good news, or have the opportunity to move ahead without His expressed guidance. Discovering His ways and how they affect our lives is a doorway to knowing His will and plan.

Men and Women Who Followed

As a young man who had been adopted into Pharaoh's family, Moses knew very little about God. Why the Lord selected him to lead His people out of captivity is a mystery—one that we cannot understand on this side of heaven. However, we certainly can see the benefits of this decision. God's choice was the right one. There is little or no evidence in Moses' young life indicating that he had a desire to know God. Yet the Lord had a plan in place. The only godly influence on Moses was his birth mother who, out of fear and in light of Pharaoh's orders to kill all male Hebrew babies, placed him in a wicker basket and set it adrift on the Nile River. The small ark floated straight into the presence of Pharaoh's daughter, who had come to the river to bathe. This woman rescued Moses and then commissioned a wet nurse to care for the baby. God placed Moses back in his mother's arms to be nursed until he grew up and was taken into Pharaoh's household (Ex. 2). God's appointments are rarely ones we would choose. I doubt any of us would have thought to save Moses' life by placing him in the care of Pharaoh's daughter, which was right in the middle of the enemy's household. But God did.

The Lord also drew David and Joseph aside in different ways, and He did the same with Ruth and Esther. Although God does not always work in the same way every time, He certainly has the motive and desire for each one of us to come to a point where we want to know Him and abide in His presence. For a short time, these men and women were separated from something or someone they cared about deeply. Only God knows why He draws a person aside, but usually it is to bring focus and spiritual depth to that one's life. He wants us to do His will, but we won't if we do not know something about His ways.

There was no way Ruth understood why her husband had to die. From a human perspective, it did not make sense. She was left alone and did not know what the future held. While God is not the author of evil or tragedy, He certainly knew the plan He had for her life. She would later meet a man named Boaz who would marry her and become the father of her son. Boaz is listed in the genealogy of Jesus Christ. In fact, Matthew records it this way: "Salmon was the father of Boaz by Rahab, Boaz was the father of Obed by Ruth, and Obed the father of Jesse. Jesse was the father of David the king" (Matt. 1:5–6). When your life is committed to Him, God can take the most devastating tragedy, the greatest loss, or the deepest sin and use it for His glory.

Esther is another example. She ended up in a very difficult situation. She was recruited as a possible replacement for Queen Vashti, who had fallen out of favor with King Ahasuerus (Est. 1). From every imaginable angle, she had no business being in the king's household. She was Jewish, and the king was Persian. Had her nationality been known, she probably would not have been chosen to remain in the king's household and to be a candidate for queen. Her situation does not make sense until we read the latter part of the book that bears her name. At a crucial point in history, God used Esther to save an entire nation from destruction—not just any nation, but His people Israel. Once again God's providence was at work.

We may not understand why He moves in a certain direction, but if we are willing to learn His ways, we will gain insight into His heart and then His Spirit will give us a desire to follow His leading, regardless of what we think should or should not happen. If you want to know the ways of God, take time—consistent time—to be alone with Him. Make a firm decision to obey Him and live your life according to His principles. If you will do this, you will be amazed at the many ways He will reveal Himself to you. But it will never be for your selfish benefit. He draws you close so that you will know Him and then make Him known to others.

You may be tempted to think that your life is broken and not usable to God. Or you may think that He is not creative enough to come up with a plan to use you for His glory. I want to assure you that He is. There may be things in your past that you feel are too dark and revealing to tell anyone. God knows all about them, and no matter what you have done, He will use you if you give your life to Him. We see this very clearly portrayed in Moses' life. There was a dramatic change the moment he learned that he was not related to Pharaoh. But even after his discovery, it was years before the Lord called to him from the burning bush.

Many people wonder, *God, can You use me? Is my life over? Will I ever reach my full potential?* Age is not a factor when God is involved. He is sovereign; His ways are perfect; and His plans are always best. No matter how old or young you are, He knows exactly where to place you so that you will learn His ways and be trained by His Spirit. He positioned Moses to become an Egyptian prince, but it was a position that he did not have very long. Once he became aware of his Hebrew heritage, Moses' allegiance began to shift. And the same should be true for you.

Once we become aware of who we are in Christ—God's beloved children—our lives should change. There should be a shift in our allegiance from that of sin and worldly things to the Savior, who is God's Son. The apostle Paul wrote: "If anyone is in Christ, he is a new creature; the old things passed away; behold, new things have come" (2 Cor. 5:17). The new thing Paul described was the spiritual new birth that we have through faith in Jesus Christ. We are born of sinful flesh, but when we accept Christ's death as atonement for our sins, we are adopted into the family of God. Our sins are forgiven and we are spiritually given the miraculous opportunity to have a personal relationship with the God of the universe.

A Difference Between the Ways and Acts of God

There is a difference between the acts of God and His ways. Moses became a witness to many of God's miraculous acts, but he also learned the ways of God. He watched as the Lord divided the waters of the Red Sea so that the nation of Israel could walk across it on dry ground. He also saw their pursuing enemies drown when he stretched out his hand in faith toward the sea (Ex. 14:26–28). "I will sing to the Lord," wrote Moses.

> For He is highly exalted;
> The horse and its rider He has hurled into the sea.
> The Lord is my strength and song,
> And He has become my salvation;
> This is my God, and I will praise Him. (Ex. 15:1–2)

He was a witness to God's mighty power on more than one occasion. Many times, when God is preparing to teach you more about Himself, He will begin by revealing one of His attributes to you in an awesome way. At another point when the nation of Israel had traveled three days without finding water, the people became frustrated. They finally came to a place named Marah, which means "bitter." It lived up to its name because the water in their region was very bitter.

So the people grumbled at Moses, saying, "What shall we drink?" Then he cried out to the Lord, and the Lord showed him a tree; and he threw it

into the waters, and the waters became sweet. There He [God] made for
them a statute and regulation, and there He tested them. And He said, "If
you will give earnest heed to the voice of the LORD your God, and do what
is right in His sight, and give ear to His commandments and keep all His
statutes, I will put none of the diseases on you which I have put on the
Egyptians; for I, the LORD, am your healer." (Ex. 15:23–26)

What was God doing by allowing them to go without water? He was
refocusing their attention from their personal need to the only One who
could meet every need they had. He said, "I, the LORD, am your healer," or
"I am the One, the only One, who can save you and provide for you." Then
He gave them a set of regulations: "If you will give earnest heed to the
voice of the LORD your God . . . . You will not experience the same diseases
that plague your enemies."

Throughout the Old Testament and even the New Testament, we continue to see God calling out to His people to turn away from sin and draw
near to Him. But they fail to do this. And for the most part people today
refuse to build an intimate relationship with Him. They go to church on
Sunday and may even think about Him and a few of His principles or
commandments during the week. But they don't move past a surface relationship and they suffer the consequences of not having close fellowship
with the Savior.

Some people become frightened at the thought of knowing God. They
believe that if they get too close, He will require something from them that
they are not ready to give. Surrendering to the Lord does not mean He will
remove every good thing from our lives. God instructed Abraham to offer
his son as a sacrifice, but it was a test of faith. The Lord stopped him the
moment He saw the depth of Abraham's faith and obedience. He always
honors our desire to obey Him. He allows our faith to be tested so that our
level of love and commitment is revealed.

Others withhold their love for God because they fear Him—but in the wrong way. It is right to stand in fearful amazement of Him, but it is wrong to fear Him from a human standpoint. The sense of awe that God commands us to have for Him is a reverent fear. When Adam and Eve sinned, they became afraid. Their act of transgression shattered their world. The extraordinary pleasure of being in God's presence was no longer theirs to experience. Sin separated them from Him, from His infinite love, along with the peace and security they once had. To some degree, we feel this same sense of anxiety whenever we disobey Him. Or we should feel something is wrong. If we don't, then our devotion to Him has grown cold. Disobedience, sin, and a feeling of doing something wrong should be enough to turn us around and cause us to go to God in prayer. If we don't, then we will want to run away from Him, which was what Adam and Eve did. God's desire is for us to understand that He is holy and worthy of all honor and praise. We fear Him not because we want to run away but because we want to honor Him with our lives.

Moses grew in his relationship with the Lord. He answered His call, but he did not know God's ways. Learning them took time, and he experienced seasons of blessing and seasons of failure. The ways of God include not only His miraculous acts and deeds but also characteristics of His nature and His attributes—He is all-powerful, all-loving, forgiving, and faithful.

One way you begin to experience intimacy with the Lord is through learning how to desire the same things that He desires for you. He wants you to love and understand His ways so you will know Him. If all you know about God is that He is all-powerful, then you really do not know very much about Him. Choosing to do good works will not make you godly inside your heart. This may look good on the surface and impress some people, but unless your heart is fully devoted to Christ, you will not experience the joy He wants you to have. The love of God at work in your life brings eternal change. When you get to a point where you say, "Lord,

I can't do this. I need You. Take my life and change me so my heart is completely Yours. I want to lay down my rights and my will to do things my way. I want to know You, and I realize that for this to take place, I must give my heart to You," then He reaches out to take your hand. He lifts you up, prepares you for His service, and gives you a greater understanding of who He is and why He is so devoted to you. The one thing you once fought against—a complete and total surrender to God—is now the very thing that brings about the greatest sense of pleasure, peace, and security.

Show Me Your Glory!

The God of the universe desires your fellowship. He created you to know Him and has placed a desire for Himself deep within your heart. When Moses showed an interest in the burning bush, God spoke to him. When Mary of Bethany sat down at the feet of Jesus, her desire for the Savior grew into a tremendous hunger which could not be satisfied by anything the world had to offer.

> As Jesus and his disciples were on their way, he came to a village where a woman named Martha opened her home to him. She had a sister called Mary, who sat at the Lord's feet listening to what he said. But Martha was distracted by all the preparations that had to be made. She came to him and asked, "Lord, don't you care that my sister has left me to do the work by myself? Tell her to help me!"
>
> "Martha, Martha," the Lord answered, "you are worried and upset about many things, but only one thing is needed. Mary has chosen *what is better*, and it will not be taken away from her." (Luke 10:38–42 NIV, *emphasis added*)

Jesus did not want to discourage Martha because He understood her desire to prepare a wonderful meal for those present. But He wanted to make a point concerning our fellowship with God. Like many of us, Martha was so distracted by her circumstances that she could not grasp the importance of *being* with the Savior. Her work and service were very important but paled in comparison to being with God. We are often guilty of doing the same thing. God's Spirit draws near, but we block His fellowship by becoming involved in countless activities.

When Jesus used the word *better*, He was talking about the fellowship she had with Him as the Messiah. A principal way that we grow in intimacy with the Savior is through reading and studying His Word. Another way is through prayer and sincere worship. A third way is by just being alone with Him. We may be in a crowded room of people, but we can experience His presence because He lives within our hearts. He is always with us. We are never alone. Though Mary was not one of the twelve disciples, she was a true follower of Christ. And she purposefully chose to sit at Jesus' feet—a position usually reserved for a disciple. What is noteworthy is that Jesus did not discourage her. While her sister was rushing around preparing the evening meal, Mary was interested in one thing, and that was Jesus.

You may have prayed, "Lord, I want to spend time with You. It never seems to work out. There is so much to do. If I take time to pray in the mornings, I'll get caught in traffic and be late to work. I can't get up any earlier because I'm too tired. I rush through each day, and when I lie down at night, I feel exhausted. I fall into bed, and the next thing I know it is time to get up and begin the routine all over again." The truth is, we cannot afford to miss time alone with God in prayer and meditation. This is where we sustain the strength and encouragement to meet the challenges of life. The psalmist wrote, "The LORD will give strength to His people; the LORD will bless His people with peace" (Ps. 29:11). And in Psalm 55:22, he stated, "Cast your burden upon the LORD and He will sustain you; He will never allow the righteous to be shaken."

Someone reading this may ask, "Are you being proud and arrogant by assuming you can know God's ways?" No, I'm just telling you that the Lord commands us to seek Him—to have a desire to know Him and His ways. He also tells us that if we will seek Him, we will find Him. The author of Proverbs wrote, "I love those who love me; and those who diligently seek me will find me" (Prov. 8:17). God loves each one of us, and I believe those who love Him deeply discover the depth of His love in ways that cannot be humanly expressed. Think about it: every woman who loves her husband wants him to know her intimately. By this I mean she wants him to know how she thinks and why she thinks a certain way. When we know someone intimately, we begin to know what that person likes, how he responds, and what he loves about us. God's acts are one thing, but His ways go much deeper. We can see His actions, but when we begin to understand why He does certain things, then we will develop true insight into God.

The Bible tells us, "The Lord used to speak to Moses face to face, just as a man speaks to his friend" (Ex. 33:11). I believe Moses developed a true understanding of God's love and acceptance. Spending time with Him in prayer teaches us about His nature and His eternal care. Then when problems come, challenges increase, or sorrows deepen, we instinctively know to go to Him for wisdom and guidance. One benefit of intimacy is trust and companionship. We walk with God and learn that He wants only the best for us. However, the moment a problem arises, some people who do not have a personal relationship with the Lord end up assuming that He is "after them" or that He wants to scold them. This often is not true. God is God. There is none like Him, and He doesn't have to stalk us to make His point or gain our attention. He may allow trouble to come as the result of sin in our lives or as a way to teach us more about Himself. If we never experience times of trouble and heartache, we would miss one of the most important aspects of God's love: His ability to comfort us when we need it the most. No one cares more for you than He does.

Moses understood he could make two requests of God: first, he wanted to know His ways, and second, he wanted to gain a deep understanding of them so he could live in close fellowship with the Lord. When I read about Moses' relationship with God, I am struck by the fact that he believed the Lord was who He said He was. And we find that Moses wanted to please Him. This is a natural part of fellowship with God. If we know we can bring joy to the life of a loved one through giving him or her something dearly cherished, we want to do it. And nothing brings more joy to God's heart than your love expressed solely to Him. You give because you have experienced a level of intimacy with Him. The very nature of God entreats us to draw close to Him. Moses prayed, "Show me Your glory!" (Ex. 33:18). He wanted to see the One who had called and accepted him.

When you love someone, you want to be with that person. Moses loved God, and he wanted to experience His fellowship. He didn't want to walk away feeling as if he knew only a couple of things about Him. He wanted to know Him. Desire, commitment, and love are requirements for understanding the ways of God. You may begin with a very simple thought about God. Yet the more you know about Him, the more you become interested in His ways. Your heart is set on encountering Him on a personal level.

Over the years, I have seen people hesitate to build a deep relationship with the Lord because they wonder what He will require of them. But once they dropped their guard and made the commitment, the pressure they once felt lifted and the feelings of conviction and guilt fell away. One thing I can tell you: I have never met a person who said, "I wish I had never obeyed the Lord." I have heard people say the opposite, but usually the comments range from "Why didn't I do this sooner?" to "I can't believe He has given me such peace." No one truly wants to stay in a rut spiritually, emotionally, or mentally.

When we express a true desire for the Lord, something inside us changes. Suddenly just going to church on Sunday is not enough. It satisfies but does not quench our thirst for God's constant care and guidance. There comes a point when we say, "I want to get on the inside of God. I want to know Him. I know He knows me, but I want to understand the depth of His knowledge." True joy and satisfaction are never found in just knowing a little about Him. They are discovered through learning His ways, walking in friendship and fellowship with Him each day, and asking Him to make His desires ours. When there is a true desire to love God, we don't settle for being in the kitchen rustling dishes around in an effort to gain approval or to be noticed. Instead, we are at the feet of Jesus—thinking of nothing but Him and how we can experience His true love and power in a more intimate way.

God Never Loses His Vision for You

In Psalm 81, God spoke to the nation of Israel through the psalmist, who wrote, "Oh that My people would listen to Me, that Israel would walk in My ways! I would quickly subdue their enemies and turn My hand against their adversaries" (vv. 13–14). God was saying, "The more you trust Me, the more I will do for you." Most of us have seen a baby bird in the nest. The moment his mother lands, he instinctively drops his head back and opens his mouth as wide as possible. He wants to get all that she has for him. God says to open your mouth wide, that is: *Expand your faith, trust Me in a big way, and watch what I will do in your life.* And I wonder if God is saying this to someone reading these words: *Oh, that you would walk in My ways. If you just knew what I had planned for you. If you understood that the best lies ahead of you. If you only realized that walking outside My ways is going to be very expensive. If you truly understood that My ways are better than your ways. If you knew that My plans and purposes are far greater than anything you could do on your own for yourself. I have all the resources at My command. I know your heart's desires. Many of these I have given to you, but to enjoy them, you must walk in My ways.*

The nation of Israel made a decision *not* to follow God, and there are times when we make that same decision. When we do, we suffer the consequences. Many times, He will step back and allow us to have our way. One terrible decision cost the Israelites an additional forty years in the wilderness and the deaths of all of the adults except Caleb and Joshua (Num. 13:25–33). Fear paralyzed their hearts and caused them to miss a divine opportunity—entry into the promised land.

You may be going through a very difficult time. Perhaps you have made a series of choices that have moved you farther and farther away from God's will. You have not chosen to walk in His ways, and this could be the very reason you are struggling emotionally, mentally, financially, and even physically. There are times when God allows us to make wrong choices because He knows that we are determined not to do His will. He will not force you to stay in a place that you have chosen to leave. It is as if the people of Israel said, "We're not going to take a step into the land. We don't care whose will it is. There are things on the other side of the border that can lead to death and discomfort, and there is no way we'll do it." I have watched people make wrong decisions, knowing there was nothing more I could do or say to change their minds.

Choice is a matter of deciding what is right according to God's plan. He has given us a limited free will. It is limited because He is sovereign. We're not. We can make choices, but ultimately God will achieve His will. If we rebel against Him, He may not use us to accomplish it, but He will do exactly what He has planned. The very reason many people struggle with depression, anxiety, and a lack of joy is that they have said no to God and stepped away from His will.

I asked one young couple who admitted that God had called them into the ministry to tell me the reason they felt they were at such a low point in their devotion to the Lord. Both agreed that something had to change, and they knew they were supposed to be in ministry work. However, they had become disgruntled with the Christian organization that hired them. Their list of what they believed were company violations against them was a long one. Some issues were valid, but the one thing they had a hard time accepting was the fact that God had not given them the freedom to leave. He had placed them in a certain position, but they felt justified in leaving. When we choose to walk away from God's plan and begin to follow our own path, we head straight into trouble. Comments such as "I feel . . ." and "What about my rights?" are earmarks of disobedience and rebellion. When we pursue our will over God's, we end up facing needless hardships and challenges. We have no true sense of peace, joy, contentment, or genuine security.

God always offers His best. He says, "I want you to walk in My way because it is the best way." This young couple balked at the idea and asked, "What about all the underhanded things we have seen take place?" I explained that unless it is totally immoral and abusive, it is still God's plan for them to stay exactly where He placed them. He is the only One who knows what the future holds. Many times, we are standing right before a door of blessings, but we want *our* way, *our* desires, and *our* rights. What happens is this: we end up missing God's very best.

Don't become entangled in Satan's web of discontentment. Difficulty will come, but as long as you are focused on obeying God, He will show you when to stay put and when to move. Israel looked at the challenge of conquering the promised land and said, "There is no way we can do this. We'll die in battle. We'll be abused. The conquest is too hard. There has to be another way!" But there is only one way to blessing, and it is God's way. He is omniscient and knows exactly what we need and when we need it.

Another thing we must remember is that He allows difficulty to teach us more about Himself. If you never came up against a trial or challenge, how could you learn about the faithfulness of God? If there was just one good moment following another one, would your faith be tested and tried? How would you recognize your spiritual growth, and more important, where would your dependence rest? It would be completely set on your ability, talent, money, connections, or any number of other things. For you to know the ways of God, you must come to a point where you release your grip on your life and circumstances. This doesn't mean that you stop being responsible. It means that you transfer your dependence from yourself to Him—the one person who knows all things, has a fantastic plan for your future, and is interested in one thing, and that is building an intimate, loving relationship with you. What could be more rewarding than knowing that He is beside you every moment leading you and guiding you through each challenge, disappointment, and victory? There is nothing compared to this.

Over my lifetime, I have known a lot of people who were very successful but did not have any peace because they did not know Jesus Christ as their Savior. Emptiness is the best way to describe their lives. Yet they fill every waking moment with activity. They don't know how to be still and just rest in God's peace. In fact, the suggestion to do this would cause a great deal of anxiety because they have spent the greater majority of their lives running away from personal hurt, the possibility of failure, and sin. They falsely believe that if they know more about God, they will reap His punishment—but nothing is farther from the truth. The fact is, the more you know about God, the more peace, joy, and love you gain. When you have Jesus, you can be alone and never be lonely because He meets your every need. All the power and fame this world has to offer cannot comfort your heart the way He does.

Knowledge Too Wonderful for Words

Are you standing at a crossroads wondering whether you can really truly trust God? You may say, "I can trust Him!" But deep inside you wonder whether you can. Israel knew about the Lord. They worshiped Him and witnessed His mighty works, but when it came down to trusting Him for something they could not see, feel, touch, or conceive happening, they failed the test. The reason I say this is that after they had spent forty years in the wilderness, God brought them back to the same spot and required the same degree of faith the second time that He did the first. This time, however, they entered the promised land.

You may be standing at the brink of a blessing, but you feel torn about the future. God understands. He knows that getting to know Him better is a process. He doesn't give us instant knowledge very often. Instead, He wants us to spend time getting to know Him and learning about His attributes and characteristics. For example, we read in His Word that He is trustworthy, but until we experience this, we won't know it on a personal level.

One way we learn more about His ways is by working through the challenges of life with Him. His ways are surprising at times, and they can be difficult to understand. Regardless they always are right. Isaiah wrote,

> "For My thoughts are not your thoughts,
> Nor are your ways My ways," declares the LORD.
> "For as the heavens are higher than the earth,
> So are My ways higher than your ways
> And My thoughts than your thoughts." (Isa. 55:8–9)

God is saying that His ways are beyond our human ability to understand them on our own. He is the One who must teach us how to know Him better. Our human minds are not wired to understand the depth and magnitude of His holy nature apart from Him. That is why He has given us His Holy Spirit. He guides us into all truth, teaches us about the heavenly Father, and provides wisdom so we will know what God wants us to do.

Once when I was out west pursuing my hobby of photography, a fellow stopped me and, within a few minutes, was trying to draw me into a heated discussion. I realized that he had seen me on television and he wanted to talk.

After a few minutes, he asked me to explain my idea of God. I knew that he really did not want to hear what I had to say; he just wanted to tell me what he believed. Finally he said, "When I can understand God and see Him, then I will trust Him." I answered, "There are some things you and I will never fully understand until we get to heaven."

Don't allow pride and arrogance to prevent you from knowing the most precious truth you will ever receive. I want to challenge you to step away from disbelief. Open God's Word and ask Him to reveal Himself to you. If you will pray, "Lord, show me Your glory. Teach me about who You are, and open my eyes so I can see You," God will do this and so much more. The man I met that day while taking photographs would not pray to receive Christ. He was angry because he wanted God to fit within the mold that he had designed and created within his mind. The Lord will never do that. His ways are surprising, powerful, righteous, and difficult at times, but they are always steady, sure, true, righteous, and awesome.

Chapter Three

YOU CAN TRUST GOD'S PROMISES

God always keeps His word. If He has given you a specific promise, you can be assured that He will fulfill it. It may not be according to your timetable, but it will always be according to what is right in line with His will for your life. A lot of people become disillusioned with God in this regard. They realize that He is leading in a certain direction and they trust Him, walk closely beside Him in faith, and believe that He is going to do what He promised. But time moves on and nothing changes. They revisit His Word day after day and reread what they believe He has spoken to them. Still, there is no change in their situation, and many times their circumstances seem to move in the opposite direction. This is when they have an opportunity to build a testimony of faith or allow their hearts to wane with thoughts of defeat.

Abraham, if he were here, would give an understanding nod to these words. He understood what it felt like to receive an irrevocable promise from the Lord. He also knew what it felt like to wait to see the fulfillment of that promise. Standing before the burning bush, Moses felt the same thing. And the disciples also knew what it felt like to have their hearts lifted by Christ's words, "I will make you fishers of men," only to later watch their Lord and Savior die one of the cruelest forms of death.

When we pray and accept His Son as our Savior, God gives us fresh hope and the eternal promise—we will be with Him one day forever. He also has promised never to leave or forsake us (John 14:18). But there are promises—words spoken to us in times of prayer and the study of His Word—that are not immediately revealed or realized.

From the confines of his prison, the prophet Jeremiah clung to a single thread of hope—that one day Israel would be released from its captivity. God gave this promise to the people. Despite this hopeful thought, however, nothing changed concerning Judah's fate. The nation remained in captivity, but the people had a promise concerning the way that God would work in the future. They had been given insight into His ways—His thinking and a glimpse of His future plan. They would be delivered, but their deliverance was based on a condition—their obedience.

> The word of the LORD came to Jeremiah the second time, while he was still confined in the court of the guard, saying, "Thus says the LORD who made the earth, the LORD who formed it to establish it, the LORD is His name, 'Call to Me and I will answer you, and I will tell you great and mighty things, which you do not know. . . . I will restore the fortunes of Judah and the fortunes of Israel and will rebuild them as they were at first. I will cleanse them from all their iniquity by which they have sinned against Me, and I will pardon all their iniquities by which they have sinned against Me and by which they have transgressed against Me.'" (Jer. 33:1–3, 7–8)

Recognizing the Importance of God's Promises

God gave Judah many promises concerning their future blessing. However, they did not grasp the importance of what God was saying. Consequently they could not understand why their circumstances did not change. Jeremiah and the remnant of people had to wait. They also had to endure severe treatment at the hands of their enemies before the promise began to unfold. God is faithful. In time, He fulfilled His promises, and He will do the same in your life. You can ask Him, "Lord, why have You allowed this to happen in my life?" He may or may not answer. However, once you begin to understand that the question is not *why* as much as it is "How do I respond, Lord?" then you will discover what so many people overlook—God's plan for their lives. Sorrow, pain, and suffering can be a part of the spiritual maturation process.

Many people do not want to wait for deliverance. They cannot look beyond their immediate need, pain, or desire and ask, "What can I gain from this experience? What does God want me to learn? What is He saying to me?" They also fail to imagine the greatness of His answers to their most intimate prayers. The people of Judah were going to be released from captivity, but the process of their release was not going to be pleasant. And isn't that what most of us want? A pleasant life with few worries, no hard times, and lots of happiness. There is nothing wrong with wanting this and God certainly wants to provide for us, but His ways are not based on what makes us happy all the time. They are based on His righteousness, faithfulness, and unconditional love for us. When we walk in His ways, we will have each of these and much more. When we decide to take a route other than His best, we suffer. But even in times of darkness, God always hears, always answers our prayers for help, and always is faithful. His promises are based on two types of declarations: absolute and conditional.

Absolute declarations are statements He makes concerning what He will do. These are things that He is going to do absolutely and totally removed from anything you may or may not do. When God says, "I will," then it is as good as done. Circumstances are not an issue. God will do what He has decided to do. Having a strong faith in His ability is crucial. There will be things that happen that you do not understand. You cannot know all that God knows, but you can learn about His ways, and rest in the fact that He is sovereign—over all things, ultimately in control, and not moved or changed by the trials and sorrows of this life. He knows what the future holds and what you need to do to face it victoriously. Worry fades when your heart is set on Him. Feelings of anxiety disappear when you realize Someone loves you with an infinite love. You may not understand how this could be true, but deep within your spirit you know that God is at work and He will not allow you to falter or fall when your heart is truly set on pleasing Him.

Conditional declarations indicate how He will act if we are obedient to Him. Moses wrote, "Now it shall be, if you *diligently* obey the LORD your God, being careful to do all His commandments which I command you today, the LORD your God will set you high above all the nations of the earth. All these blessings will come upon you and overtake you if you obey the LORD your God" (Deut. 28:1–2, *emphasis added*). The key word in these two verses is *diligently*. God wants us to seek Him with diligence, but many times we come to Him only when we need something. Instead, we must seek Him with a trueness of heart and mind—wanting to know Him because He created us and has given us life. Israel could not quite make this mental connection, and many people today cannot either. We become busy or end up feeling as though our problems and circumstances are more important than doing what God has commanded us to do. But He deliberately instructed the people to "diligently obey the LORD," and if they did, then they would receive His blessing. He was giving them a conditional declaration. There are some things that God will do no matter what we do. Then there are things that He will do only if we act according to His ways and principles.

A similar principle is this: we reap what we sow, more than we sow, and later than we sow. But this does not stop some from disobeying God. They do not believe there are consequences to their decisions just because, for the moment, they are experiencing a sense of happiness. They believe that somehow they will escape or bypass the consequences of their sin. Therefore, they continue to commit all kinds of evil—drifting further from God by yielding to wickedness, disobedience, and vile things that absolutely destroy them. With each step they take, they tell themselves, "Nothing is going to happen to me. I won't get caught." The bottom line is this: they do not believe the simple truth of God's Word. They don't take Him seriously.

When you and I take Him seriously, we are going to believe that He will do what He says He will do. When He says, "I will," then without exception He will do it. When He says, "I will bless you if you obey Me," He will do what He says. When He tells you, or when you sense a serious check in your spirit and you know that what you are about to do is not in keeping with His will for your life, then you can expect to experience His judgment. The nation of Israel did not seize the opportunity and enter the promised land the first time God led them to a point where they could claim His promise as their own. However, the second time they approached the land, they went in without argument or hesitation (Josh. 3:1–4).

God is our awesome God of love, blessing, joy, and peace. One of His greatest joys is to give us our hearts' desires. But when He says, "Thou shalt not," He means *don't do it if you want to experience My love, protection, and blessings.* I realize that a lot of people sit in church week after week listening to sermons and hearing His truth only to walk out of the sanctuary and continue to disobey Him. In their disobedience, they are saying, "I don't really believe that He will punish me. He is the God of love, goodness, and mercy. He doesn't do bad things to us." The truth is, if we disobey Him, He will allow us to experience the consequences that accompany our disobedience.

The Acid Pain of Sin

People who yield to temptation may say, "I'm not hurting anyone else." But this is not true. Sin has a ripple effect that stretches out and touches the lives of those we love. God is faithful to warn us not to pursue a sinful course of action. If we persist, He will allow us to continue and He will even step aside because He knows the determination of our wills. He doesn't want us to yield to sin, but He has given us a limited free will. That is, while He is ultimately sovereign over all things, He created us to make choices: good and bad. We can choose to disobey God or to do the opposite of what we know is right. We also can allow our feelings to become so dominant that we can no longer sense God's guidance through the Holy Spirit. I encourage people to pray and ask God to give them a scripture to cling to when their faith is challenged instead of responding and reacting immediately to the situation. If God says "go," you can remind Him of His personal promise to you when trials come and you wonder whether you have made the right choice. Don't just open the Bible and claim the first promise you see because it could be dead wrong.

Take time to pray and lay out the matter before the Lord. He knows your heart, and He realizes the depth of your feelings. When you learn His ways, doing this will not seem very difficult. Instead of wishing you had a quick answer, you will begin to look forward to your time spent in prayer seeking His wisdom and guidance. Prayer does not automatically change our circumstances. God is motivated by our words, but He is not forced into action. Instead, prayer—time spent in His presence—changes us.

Moses walked away from the burning bush experience with a totally different perspective of God. He had heard of God. But after being in His presence, Moses was never the same. He did not look at life the same way. Then after God delivered the nation of Israel from the Egyptians, he no longer viewed obstacles as impossible. Did Moses make mistakes in the future? Yes. And you will too. But God wants you to learn from your mistakes.

God's goal in teaching you about His ways is to draw you near to Himself. He knows there will be times when you fail. However, He wants to mold and shape your life so that your character reflects His godly influence. Each time you pick up His Word or pray, there is a great potential for spiritual growth. God cannot lie. He tells us that if we call to Him, He will answer us and "tell [us] great and mighty things, which [we] do not know" (Jer. 33:3). We can claim this promise that also reflects the nature of God: He desires to reveal Himself to us. We can know His ways, but we must seek Him. He tells us that when we do, we will find Him (2 Chr. 15:4).

Nonnegotiable: The Consequences of Sin

The Lord gave Adam and Eve a clear warning. He said, "From the tree of the knowledge of good and evil you shall not eat, for in the day that you eat from it you will surely die" (Gen. 2:17). Notice that He did not say, "If you do this, then this is what will happen." He knew what was going to happen, and He was already laying the foundation for their redemption. The fact that He walked through the garden of Eden as if to search for the ones He had created was really for our benefit. Adam and Eve heard His call. They disobeyed a very simple plan of God, and He was about to reveal the source of the problem, which was sin. It was a sad ending to a promising beginning.

He created us to need Him

Separation from God

There was an immediate sense of separation from His fellowship. The moment Adam heard God's voice calling to him, he realized something was wrong, so he hid. Broken fellowship is one of the most difficult things we can experience, especially when the person we have known as a friend was dearly loved. This is why separation from God is so devastating. He created us to know and love Him. He wired us for fellowship with Himself and with others. But if we allow sin to enter our lives, then our fellowship with the loving God of the universe is broken, and we know it. Deep in our hearts and souls, we ache when we cannot pray or talk with Him without thinking about our sin. The even sadder truth is that over time, we can actually become numb or callous to sin and never notice or consider what we are missing by denying His friendship.

Adam had never been separated from God. It was not until he disobeyed the Lord that his life became gripped by a gnawing sense of separation that continued to grow within his heart and mind. But God in His mercy and grace did not abandon him. We can experience unbroken fellowship with God through Jesus Christ, His Son. We do not have to live in a state of separation. When we yield to sin and sense the separation that comes through disobedience, we can seek God's forgiveness and know that He will restore us.

Sense of Shame

A sense of shame filled Adam's and Eve's hearts. They did not understand guilt and conviction immediately. They hid from God because their consciences revealed that something was wrong. Perhaps they did not even know what they were feeling. All they knew was that when they heard God's voice, they wanted to hide.

Consider how many people are hiding today because of the sin in their lives. Some have grown up in Christian homes and know what is right and what is wrong, but they have chosen to disobey God's law and are suffering because of their decisions. Psychologists—Christian and secular—know the effect of guilt on our lives. The moment we violate our moral compass, an alarm sounds inside us. If we do not heed the warning and we keep pressing forward—against what we know is right—we will sense an increase of emotional stress, which can lead to other problems, some of which are very serious.

Think of all the people Jesus loved and accepted. He never turns anyone away. When we come to Him, He accepts us. He has perfect knowledge. He knew what Adam and Eve had done, but He had a plan for the rest of their lives. His will was not altered. Their need for forgiveness became a catalyst for the salvation of mankind. God's eternal plan for us began to unfold at this point, and we do not have to be afraid to come to Him seeking His forgiveness and restoration. His mercy and grace—freely given—dissolves sin's deepest shadows.

Pride

Pride was exposed. Satan's temptation included a very wicked hook. He told Adam and Eve that if they ate of the tree, they would not die but, in fact, would become like God. How many times have you heard the voice of pride whisper: "Do this and others will notice. You will be recognized for your potential—after all, no one seems to be noticing it now. But if you push ahead, raise some awareness, and make others look a little inept, you will gain the boss's attention and you will be rewarded handsomely for your efforts"? But you never are.

Satan's lies are full of vain ideas. Anytime there is a push to bypass the commands of God, we can bank on trouble appearing because we always reap what we sow, more than we sow, and later than we sow. Although God's love for Adam did not wane, that did not stop or prevent the consequences of sin in his life. He disobeyed Him and had to face what he had done. His pride was revealed. God turned the lights on and exposed the darkness of his deed. Pride is the very thing that most believers battle through life. Though we love the Lord, the enemy never tires of propositioning us into disobeying the Lord. Therefore, we need to ask God to make us sensitive to Satan's ploys, or we will continue to face one spiritual defeat after another.

Death

Ultimately there was death. There is a spiritual death and a physical death. The first of these Adam experienced immediately following his act of disobedience. Up to the point where he succumbed to temptation, he was eternally alive with God. Spiritually, emotionally, and mentally he was in tune with the Lord. Physically he was not subject to disease, hunger, or any of the physical problems we face today. All his needs were perfectly met. Then why did he sin? When God created man, He gave him a limited free will. That is, He has given us the ability to choose right from wrong. He is sovereign and ultimately over all things, but He also wants us to make a choice to love, honor, worship, and obey Him. What good can be gained if He forces us to love Him? God is not honored with obligation. He is honored by our desire to obey simply because we know His way is best, and we also understand that He loves us.

Death is sin's punishment—and this is not a part of God's plan for mankind—but we can certainly choose to deny Him and face that ending to life. However, for those who accept Christ as Savior and Lord, life does not end when physical death comes. God sent His Son, the Lord Jesus Christ, to earth to overcome this very thing. Through faith in Him, we are given eternal life. Though He was crucified, He rose from the grave and is alive today in us through the power and presence of the Holy Spirit. When we disobey Him, we grieve His heart. Paul cautioned us not to do this: "Do not grieve the Holy Spirit of God, by whom you were sealed for the day of redemption" (Eph. 4:30).

You may ask, "If Adam and Eve—created by God and chosen to live in a perfect environment—deliberately, willfully chose to disobey God, are the consequences of their sin still in operation?" The answer is yes. For now, we live in a fallen world. Separation, shame, suffering, and death are the consequences of the first couple's sin. God has not changed His law. But here is where God's ways are not our ways. He has made provision for our sin. Not so we can continue living in disobedience, but so we can experience His forgiveness and restoration. Life on this earth will never be perfect the way it was in the beginning, but we can have perfect love living inside us through faith in Christ. We also can be assured that one day, we will walk with Him in perfect peace, love, joy, and contentment when we are with Him in heaven. However, even now we can enjoy these by drawing nearer to Him, learning His ways, and resting in His presence.

Keeping a Promise

What do you do when you know God has made a promise, but any sign of its fulfillment appears no closer than when He first gave it to you months or even years ago? Noah is an extreme example of having faith in God's promises. In Genesis we read,

> The LORD saw that the wickedness of man was great on the earth, and that every intent of the thoughts of his heart was only evil continually. The LORD was sorry that He had made man on the earth, and He was grieved in His heart. The LORD said, "I will blot out man whom I have created from the face of the land, from man to animals to creeping things and to birds of the sky; for I am sorry that I have made them." But Noah found favor in the eyes of the LORD. . . .
>
> Then God said to Noah, "The end of all flesh has come before Me; for the earth is filled with violence because of them; and behold, I am about to destroy them with the earth. Make for yourself an ark of gopher wood; you . . . shall cover it inside and out with pitch. . . . Behold, I, even I am bringing the flood of water upon the earth, to destroy all flesh in which is the breath of life, from under heaven; everything that is on the earth shall perish. But I will establish My covenant with you; and you shall enter the ark—you and your sons and your wife, and your sons' wives with you." (6:5–8, 13–14, 17–18)

The ark was not constructed in a week or even several months. It took a tremendous amount of time and effort to build the floating structure. Every swing of Noah's ax as he chopped and fitted the vessel's gopher wood planks was a practicum of faith. Every scoop of hot pitch that was applied to the ark was done because the Lord had instructed him to do so. He also realized that once the ark was completed, the work had only just begun. Then it had to be filled with animals and adequate provisions stored away for everyone's and everything's survival.

In fulfilling his mission, Noah never hesitated or asked for God to give him a sign that he was doing the right thing. He knew it. He had not missed what the Lord was saying. The only decision that needed to be made was one of obedience, and Noah never considered anything but obedience. Some scholars estimate the ark was at least six stories high and as long as two football fields. It was a flat-bottomed vessel and was built without a thought as to how it would cut through crashing waves or be steered. But Noah was not worried; God was the Captain. It was an ark—a floating barge that was cradled in His providential care.

Regardless of what others said or thought about him, Noah stayed on the course that had been plotted for him to follow. While construction continued for years, Satan used the prolonged process to weave his deceptive web, tempting God's servant to become discouraged and stop the building process. But Noah never did. On more than one occasion, he probably had to remind himself of the Lord's words and particularly His promise. The flood would come. It would be a reality, and his family would survive.

The Bible says, "Noah did according to all that the LORD had commanded him" (Gen. 7:5). God's ways are faithful. They never fail. Even so, many times we do not respond accordingly to His promise of provision. Noah did, however. The psalmist asserted, "Your kingdom is an everlasting kingdom, and your dominion endures through all generations. The LORD is faithful to all his promises and loving toward all he has made" (Ps. 145:13 NIV).

Just as God promised, a deluge of rain began to fall for forty days and nights. Finally it stopped, but Noah and his family had to wait even longer before they experienced the fullness of God's promise. The water did not recede for months. Therefore, day in and day out the ark floated along without a hint of land in sight:

In the seventh month, on the seventeenth day of the month, the ark rested upon the mountains of Ararat. The water decreased steadily until the tenth month; in the tenth month, on the first day of the month, the tops of the mountains became visible. Then it came about at the end of forty days, that Noah opened the window of the ark which he had made; and he sent out a raven, and it flew here and there until the water was dried up from the earth. Then he sent out a dove from him, to see if the water was abated from the face of the land; but the dove found no resting place for the sole of her foot, so she returned to him into the ark, for the water was on the surface of all the earth. Then he put out his hand and took her, and brought her into the ark to himself. So he waited yet another seven days; and again he sent out the dove from the ark. The dove came to him toward evening, and behold, in her beak was a freshly picked olive leaf. So Noah knew that the water was abated from the earth. Then he waited yet another seven days, and sent out the dove; but she did not return to him again. (Gen. 8:4–12)

If you are waiting for the promise God has made to you to unfold, don't give up. At the beginning of this chapter in Genesis, we read that "God remembered Noah and all the beasts and all the cattle that were with him in the ark; and God caused a wind to pass over the earth, and the water subsided" (v. 1). "God remembered Noah," and He will not forget you. His ways are faithful, His promises sure, and though you may find yourself waiting for an indefinite period of time, continue to do so because when the answer comes, it will be worth it all. Pushing, manipulating circumstances, and calculating what you can do next in order to get God to respond to your relentless requests are wastes of time. Noah used extreme wisdom as he waited throughout the years. Notice what he did not do:

He did not badger God for an explanation. He never asked *why*. Noah just obeyed God, and this speaks volumes about his character and faith in God: "Thus Noah did; according to all that God had commanded him, so he did" (Gen. 6:22).

He did not argue with God over whether he should do the work or not. Noah knew he was not equal to the task. He was not the head of a successful construction company. There were no extreme-makeover teams waiting in the wings to take over and complete the construction should he fail. We can imagine that month after month as the building process progressed, so did the comments from extended family members and friends. None were available to help, and he did not ask. He just kept doing what he had been given to do because he knew what God had said He would do—and he believed Him.

He did not become discouraged, even though the process took years. It is evident that Noah understood something about God's ways, and that is this: He will do exactly what He has said. While Noah was not perfect or sinless, he found favor in God's eyes—perhaps because he was willing to trust the great I AM with his life and the lives of those he loved. His entire life was caught up in one thing: obedience to God.

Learning to Trust at a Deeper Level

Years ago, I got up on a Sunday morning and was getting ready to go to church when I became overwhelmed by a problem that I was facing. It was much more than I could handle on my own. Up to that point, I had prayed and felt the Lord saying, *Just trust Me*, but the impact this was having on my life was tremendous. I could not escape it, and I did not know how I would get through it. I walked into my bedroom and got down beside my bed and prayed and began to cry out to God. "Why don't You just get on with this?" I heard myself say. Just like all of us do at times, I had become impatient. I remember kneeling and struggling and weeping a little bit. You know how God speaks to you, and I know how He speaks to me. He could not have made this any clearer.

All of a sudden, I sensed Him whisper to me, *You can trust perfect love.* When He said that, my burden lifted immediately—my frustration and anxiety disappeared. I got up, finished dressing, and continued preparing for the day. Ever since then, my understanding of God's love and His ways in times of waiting took a huge step forward. I realized that God, who loves me without end, was saying, "My love for you is trustworthy in any and every situation you encounter in life." I may not understand why He allows some things to happen, but I can trust Him. There is no other conclusion. Moses stood in His presence and came away convinced that God was exactly who He said He was. He did not know how he would be used to lead Israel to the threshold of the promised land; he just knew he had to do what he was given to do. That was the end of the discussion. We need to obey God on the basis of who is doing the talking. Perfect love is trustworthy, and this is the only kind of love that God knows.

Someone reading this may be thinking, *God has never spoken to me. How can I know His ways when I can't even hear His voice?* I want you to understand that He has spoken to you. If you are a believer, He spoke to you when He convicted you of your sin and showed you that you needed to be saved. When you were tempted to doubt your salvation or His love for you, but read in His Word about how He loves you with an everlasting love and how He died on the cross for your sins, you were hearing the voice of God. He speaks to us through His Word, through the presence of the Holy Spirit who lives inside every believer, and through godly men and women. The only time we should sense God being silent in a distant sort of way is when we have deliberately sinned against Him. We may not hear His voice in every waking moment. He speaks to our hearts when we need to hear what He has to say. But there should be a warmth burning inside us that reminds us of His intimate care.

You may even wonder whether He is aware of your needs. I assure you He is. You cannot allow your feelings to govern how you view God's ways and His goodness. There was a point when Sarah doubted she would have a son. God had given her husband, Abraham, a promise, but as time had moved on, she failed to see how it would be fulfilled. God specializes in miracles. When it appeared there was no way for Him to do what He had promised, the Lord appeared to Abraham and reminded him that He had not forgotten what He said:

Now the LORD appeared to him by the oaks of Mamre, while he was sitting at the tent door in the heat of the day. When [Abraham] lifted up his eyes and looked, behold, three men were standing opposite him; and when he saw them, he ran from the tent door to meet them and bowed himself to the earth, and said, "My lord, if now I have found favor in your sight, please do not pass your servant by." . . . So Abraham hurried into the tent to Sarah, and said, "Quickly, prepare three measures of fine flour, knead it and make bread cakes." . . . He took curds and milk and the calf which he had prepared, and placed it before them. . . . Then they said to him, "Where is Sarah your wife?" And he said, "There, in the tent." He said, "I will surely return to you at this time next year; and behold, Sarah your wife will have a son." And Sarah was listening at the tent door, which was behind him. Now Abraham and Sarah were old, advanced in age; Sarah was past childbearing. Sarah laughed to herself, saying, "After I have become old, shall I have pleasure, my lord being old also?" And the LORD said to Abraham, "Why did Sarah laugh . . . ? Is anything too difficult for the LORD? At the appointed time I will return to you, at this time next year, and Sarah will have a son." Sarah denied it however, saying, "I did not laugh"; for she was afraid. And He said, "No, but you did laugh." (Gen. 18:1–3, 6, 8–15)

Simply said: Sarah did not believe God would keep His promise. But He always does. If He tells you that He will do something or if you truly sense that He has a plan that involves some portion of your future, you need to be watchful, trusting, and patient as you wait for it to unfold. Sarah did not do this. She talked Abraham into having a child by her maidservant, and the Middle East is still in turmoil today as a result of her unfaithful decision. Ishmael is the father of Islam.

Notice what God did when Sarah decided to take matters into her own hands. He did not prevent her from doing what she was determined to do. Even so, He proved faithful. He fulfilled His promise according to His timetable and not according to what Sarah felt was best. Have you ever pushed past and ahead of God and wished you had never done it? Most of us have. We also keenly know far too well what it feels like to regret what we have done. When we don't have all the facts, we need to wait for God to show us the next step. No matter how difficult this seems, it is better to wait in faith than to move forward and end up making a wrong decision and regretting what has happened.

I Want to Hear Your Voice!

Sarah could not undo what she had done. She had to live with the consequences, but that did not cause God to withhold His blessing. When you go through an emotional valley, remember that God never changes. He has declared His unconditional love for you, and even though you feel you have made a huge mistake, God still loves you and He will never forsake you or turn His back on you. What he will do is reject your sinfulness. You can choose to walk away from Him, but He will never walk away from you. If you are not hearing God's voice, ask Him to show you if you have moved away from Him. Also, pray that He will make it clear if you are believing the enemy's lies—words that tell you that you have disappointed the Lord and there is no way He will take time to talk with you. In order to hear God, you must believe some basic truths.

1) He Loves You

The greatest verse concerning God's love for you is one you know by heart: "For God so loved the world, that He gave His only begotten Son, that whoever believes in Him shall not perish, but have eternal life" (John 3:16). The Lord made a conscious decision to come to earth to demonstrate His love for you by living and identifying with your every need. But His love did not stop there. He died for your sins. He did what you could not do for yourself. He became the atonement for every transgression—past, present, and future—that you will commit. There is no greater love than the love God has for you.

2) He Enjoys Being with You

The Bible tells us that God rejoices over us: "As the bridegroom rejoices over the bride, so your God will rejoice over you" (Isa. 62:5). Even though this verse is spoken to Israel, it demonstrates the nature and character of our loving God who finds delight in those who love and honor Him.

3) He Has a Plan for Your Life

No matter how young or old you are or how many mistakes you have made, there are no hopeless cases in God's eyes. When He looks at your life, He sees only potential. You may ask, "Doesn't He keep a record of all that I have done wrong?" He doesn't have to. He is God, and He is omniscient. He knows all that you will do in the future. The past is behind you, but the future is in front of you. You can make a decision right now to live the rest of your life doing what God gives you to do and enjoy His blessings. Or you can resist Him, chase your own dreams, and more than likely fall short of your potential.

Moses committed a hideous crime: he murdered another man. But after he had suffered the consequences of his rash actions, God began to work in his life—molding him and preparing him for future service. If you asked Moses, "Did you ever think that God could use you after you had jumped ahead of Him and acted so unwisely?" he probably would say no. In such situations, God pulls back the veil of our humanity so we can grasp the depth of His unfailing love and commitment. Moses was still the man God wanted to lead His people out of Egypt. And the same is true when it comes to you and your future. His overall plan has not changed. Sin may alter the way He unfolds His plan in your life, but He will never abandon the works of His hands (Ps. 138:8).

Knowing God's Ways Prepares Us for the Future

We mistakenly think, *If I could just make more money, everything would be better*, but it never is because God wants our focus to be on Him and not on our income. He knows the direction we need to take to accomplish the goals He has set for us. Many things we do each day fall within His will. But when our desire and motivation are set on selfish gain just so we can say we have more, we are not living to our fullest or living the way He wants us to live. Essentially we are settling for much less than we could have if we surrendered our lives and allowed Him to guide us.

Moses reached this conclusion after hearing that God had chosen him to lead Israel out of Egyptian bondage. God is always very explicit in His instruction: "The LORD said to Moses, 'When you go back to Egypt see that you perform before Pharaoh all the wonders which I have put in your power;

but I will harden his heart so that he will not let the people go'" (Ex. 4:21). At these words, most of us may have wanted to say, "Wait a minute, Lord. I thought You just said that You 'have surely seen the affliction of My people who are in Egypt.' If you 'harden' Pharaoh's heart, then he will never let the people leave and they will remain in bondage. I'm wasting my time trying to lead them out of the land."

God was in the process of opening Moses' eyes to the reality of his situation and also preparing him for what would take place. We do not have infinite knowledge, but the Lord does. He knew exactly why He was going to cause Pharaoh to be resistant and refuse to let the nation of Israel go. Moses, however, had to deal with this situation based on the fact that God was sovereign and knew what He was doing. In fact, He was laying out His plan before Moses to follow.

God had given him insight into what was going to happen. He often will do the same for us. When He does, it is our responsibility to trust Him and not look at our surroundings and question His ability. The storm may be raging, as it was with the disciples on the Sea of Galilee (Matt. 8:23-27). Still, we must keep God's faithfulness at the center of our thoughts. When He calls us to do something, He provides the strength we need and the way to get it done.

From a human perspective, the task seemed impossible. Miraculously God called to Moses from the burning bush. Many times, the way He speaks to us will be right in line with the mission He gives us to do. He had to get Moses' attention, and speaking from the burning bush was the way He chose to do it. It worked because Moses never forgot what it felt like to stand in the Lord's presence. Often God will work in our lives in such a way that we will know that He is acting and we cannot deny it. Then, later, when our faith is challenged, we will recall what He has done, and we will stay the course rather than yield to feelings of doubt and fear.

The plan required faith. God will open a door of opportunity, but He will not push us through it. We must step forward. When we do, we will sense His presence clearing the way for us to travel forward. And there may even be a time when we do what David did; we "walk through the valley of the shadow of death, [discouragement, or hopelessness]" without becoming fearful because we know that He is with us every step of the way (Ps. 23:4).

Moses prayed to the Lord,

"If Your presence does not go with us, do not lead us up from here. For how then can it be known that I have found favor in Your sight, I and Your people? Is it not by Your going with us, so that we . . . may be distinguished from all the other people who are upon the face of the earth?"

The Lord said to Moses, "I will also do this thing of which you have spoken; for you have found favor in My sight and I have known you by name." (Ex. 33:15–17)

It takes faith to ask the Lord to make His presence known or, if nothing else, to reaffirm that what you are doing is right in step with His plan. When He makes His will clear, you step forward by faith and you keep moving until He says, "Stop." Even if you are tempted to become fearful, the enemy will scatter as you proclaim your faith and obedience to God. He cannot stand the thought of your honoring the Lord with your life.

God answered Israel's prayers. Even though the people stumbled in their walk with God, He continued loving them. He had a plan for their lives that was much greater than they could imagine. While they were fussing around trying to decide if they would follow Moses and obey God, the Lord just kept moving them out of their comfort zone. They would be released from bondage, and this would come about as a result of His mercy and grace at work in their lives. We must also remember that God's plan for man's redemption is at work throughout history. Each event, every word written in the Bible leads to one conclusion: God loves us, and He sent His

Son to earth to die for us so that we might come to know Him and have eternal life. Today, we gain freedom from bondage not by willing ourselves to be free, but by placing our faith in the person of Jesus Christ—the only One who can deliver us from all sin and fear.

Promises Fulfilled Based on Obedience

Recently during our men's prayer breakfast, I heard a testimony from a young man who said God had made it very clear that he needed to quit his job. He said that he double-checked with the Lord in prayer because nothing at his workplace seemed wrong. However, he followed the Lord's leading, and he quit. A short time later, an opportunity opened up that, had he been at his other job, he never would have noticed. The next thing he knew, he was receiving a salary several times more than what he was making with his previous employer. He simply waited a short period of time for God to work. The key to the blessing was his obedience. He did not understand all the *whys* and *why-nots*. He just knew to step forward, trusting that God knew much more than he could see or imagine.

Many times, we cannot wait until we see everything perfectly. God may never give us all the details behind His plan and purpose for our lives. In fact, often He reveals to us only what we need to know at the moment. Later, we may conclude why certain things turned out the way they did. We can see His hand of blessing at work even in the aftermath of extreme difficulty. However, in the heat of battle when feelings of disappointment, grief, or shock are raging within us, we may be able to do only one thing, and that is to trust Him.

Moses certainly did not have all the details given to him up front. He had to take one day, one month, one year, and one event at a time. He couldn't ask the Lord to give him a rundown on why the nation was being chased into the depths of the Red Sea; he simply had to trust and go forward. There will be times when God calls you to do the same—go forward by faith. God's promise to the people of Israel was based on their obedience. He wanted them to go forward and to trust Him for what seemed to be impossible. You can apply this same principle to your life. When you feel as though you are facing the Red Sea of hopelessness, ask God to make a way for you to travel through the difficulty. Then trust Him. I can assure you of this: you will always come out ahead by placing your faith in God and His ability to work on your behalf. Remember, the waters of the sea did not part until the priest walked into it. In other words, the people had to demonstrate their faith in a sovereign and holy God. Once they did this, the way before them opened up and they walked on dry land.

I have faced many challenges when there was only one thing I could do and that was to trust God. There are two occasions when this truth stands out in my memory. The first was when I chose to obey the Lord and move my family to Atlanta, Georgia, in the fall of 1969. After spending a great deal of time in prayer, I sensed God saying, *Here is what I'm going to do.* He did not say *if, and,* or *but.* He said, *This is what I'm going to do.* There was no room for argument. I knew He had spoken to me, and the issue was settled. He had a plan in mind and my only course of action was to obey Him. If I had resisted, the outcome would have been costly to my ministry. The second time had to do with the broadcast ministry of In Touch. Once again, He told me: *Here is what I'm going to do. Trust Me!* In both situations, God never said, *My decision is up for review. Tell me what you think.* He motivated me to draw near to Him, and then He shaped my will so that it fit perfectly with His plan for my life. He didn't even prompt me to pray because that was what I wanted to do most—pray and learn more about His plans. I did not want to miss what He was doing.

Both times God prepared my heart for what was ahead. I had studied His Word, listened for His voice of instruction, and opened my heart to His principles. Then when it was time for Him to turn me in a certain direction, I was ready. I didn't worry about having or not having a choice. That was not an issue. What was primary in my mind was being in a position to be blessed by Him because obedience always leads to blessing. Will God do the same thing in your life? Yes. If it is something crucial that has the potential to affect your future, He will do this same thing for you. When I think about the people who say, "No, Lord, I'm not going to do that," I feel very badly because I know they have missed an opportunity to obey God, receive His blessings, and position themselves for greater service. If I had said, "No, I'm not going to move from this place. I love living near the beach. So, just forget it, God," I would have missed doing what He created me to do all these years.

There will be times when we say no to God and miss a very important opportunity. It may even be the opportunity of a lifetime. Does this mean He can never use us again? No. At whatever point we say, "Lord, here I am," He will take us and use us in ways that are beyond our ability to understand. Never underestimate what God will do in your life. Be willing to learn, to listen, and to start obeying Him in the simple things. Then when you come to crucial decisions, you will know how to watch for His ways and respond correctly. Maybe you have never trusted Jesus Christ as your Savior, and you can give me several convincing reasons why you don't think He will save you. A few years ago an older man told me, "I have been wild all of my life. I'm an alcoholic, and I have treated people badly. I'm unfit to live with God, and there is no way He would keep a single promise to a person like me." But He does. God longs to bless and use us for His glory. Jesus said, "The one who comes to Me I will certainly not cast out" (John 6:37). He loves us no matter how grave our sin or rebellion may appear. When He sent His Son to die on the cross, He proclaimed to the world His unconditional love for you. And if you will ask Him to forgive your sins based on His Son's atoning death, He will do it. He will forgive you, cleanse you, and mold you into a person whose life contains great eternal potential. One day you will reign with Him in heaven forever. You may not understand how this can possibly be true, but it is. When you begin to understand the way God operates, you will sense His eternal care surrounding you and, as He did with Moses, guiding you each step of the way.

Chapter Four

THE WAYS GOD REVEALS HIMSELF

Have you ever seriously thought about the way God works in your life? His acts are not random. Each event and every lesson are parts of a grander plan. Even in times that we deem as being almost insignificant, God is at work in a marvelous way. When I became interested in photography, I was amazed at God's awesome creation. I noticed all the big things—snow-capped mountains, glaciers, picturesque waterfalls, gigantic waves breaking on the rocky shores of northern California, misty forests, towering redwoods, and acres and acres of beautiful flowers. I was caught up in the big things. But then I trained myself to move closer to my subject, and an entirely different world opened before me. I began to see another side of God's beauty. Instead of photographing a whole field of flowers, I got inside just one. I saw the most awesome thing—God's delicate, intricate, detailed creation. The same is true about knowing Him, only on a much grander scale. The closer we get to Him, the better we understand His ways. Life has dimension. It is not flat or broad without color. There is depth, and there is joy.

I remember on one occasion when my granddaughter was only ten, I thought about asking her to go with me to take some pictures in the backyard of the house next door to hers. I said, "Annie, you want to go with Gimps [her name for me] photographing?" She quickly answered, "I sure do." We walked next door together, and as I set up the camera, she walked around looking at all the beautiful flowers. After I scanned the area, I decided to take a close-up picture of this absolutely beautiful flower that was in full bloom. I purposefully placed the camera on a tripod at a lower level so I could show her what I was doing. I focused deep inside the flower and could see the finest details. Then I asked her to look through the camera's view-finder. I will never forget the expression on her face. She said, "Wow, Gimps!" From that moment on, I never had to ask her if she wanted to come with me. She was hooked on photography with one look.

The same thing happened when I was out west with friends. We were in two cars, and as we went around a bend in the road, a huge field of flowers greeted us. I was amazed by the sight and decided to stop and photograph the scene, but not the way my friend's wife thought it should be done. She watched as I walked down into the field and set up my camera so that I could photograph this one particular flower. After a few minutes, she walked down to where I was working and asked, "Why are you taking so much trouble to get your equipment out of the vehicle and come down this hill and set everything up? You could just take the picture, and it would be very nice." By this point, my camera was set up, and I asked her to look at the photo that I planned to take. She bent over and looked through the camera's lens. Immediately she looked up at me and said, "Okay, now I understand. I can see what you're doing."

The View from the Inside of God's Love

While our knowledge of God is limited, the closer we become to Him the more understanding we will gain. Like a photograph of a vast landscape, it is awe-inspiring, but it does not reveal what is going on in the hidden corners—the places where light filters in, bringing warmth and a sense of belonging. If we hold God at a distance, we will never know the way He operates, thinks, or loves. Why does a person's faith seem small at times? The answer is very simple: he or she does not know or understand the depth of love that God has for him or her. By *know*, I mean *experience*. We can experience His love on such a personal level that our hearts become set on one thing—knowing Him to an even greater degree.

You can have all your heart longs to have through a personal relationship with Jesus Christ. What can possibly be better than this? There is just no denying it: if you want to live life to the fullest, draw near to God and allow Him to draw close to you. Satan does not want you to do this. And he will do anything to prevent you from experiencing the goodness of God. He knows that once you do—once you get a closer look at what He has for you—you will stop settling for second best, third, or much less. While the enemy drums up one distraction after another, God remains steady and unshaken in His devotion to you.

False guilt is one of Satan's favorite weapons. He loves to accuse and blame us for things that God does not even take time to consider. He also seeks to engage us in self-centered thoughts about our futures, dreams, perceived rights, and needs. When we fail to spend time with God in prayer or the study of His Word, the enemy quickly chides us with thoughts of guilt that dog our every step, telling us that there is no way we can possibly love the Lord. No matter how much we try, he pushes his relentless lies upon us, saying that our lives will never count and because of our past failure, God does not have anything for us to do that will count in eternity.

If you have been listening to lies like these and more, stop. Right now, stop listening, and begin opening your heart to the truth of God's Word. If you really want to know the way He operates, this is where you will discover it. God wants you to know Him intimately so you can stand against the enemy's lies. But if you never pray, go to church, or read His Word, you will be defenseless under the enemy's attack.

Remember in an earlier chapter we discussed the world's view of intimacy, which usually involves sexual contact. But this is a distortion of what God created intimacy to be. We are intimate physically with our spouses, but there also is an intimacy that goes beyond any form of physical contact. You can have an intimate friend—someone who knows all there is to know about you and loves you without regret or hesitation. That is intimacy in a very deep form.

People who are intimate with each other can be together without feeling the need to fill all the gaps of silence with conversation. It is enough to be together. You may not even be in the presence of the person you love, but because of an unspoken intimacy between the two of you, you have a bond of love that cannot be broken. Godly, loving intimacy bonds us with those we love. As we also said, it is essential to every long-standing relationship, and it is especially true when it comes to our relationship with God. If we find it difficult to open up to Him, then we will not live within the realm of intimacy that He wants us to know and enjoy.

The deeper truth is that if we cannot be intimate with Him, we won't know how to be intimate with others—spouses, friends, and family members. We'll be able to go only so deep but never to the depth that brings healing and a sense of unimaginable trust. Of course, God is our dearest friend. There are things that we can tell Him that no one else will understand. I can say, "Lord, You know how I feel," and realize that He does! Even though He allows and encourages me to express my feelings of joy, sorrow, and disappointment, He knows it all. And really, the most we have to do, especially when we are hurting, is to bow our hearts in His presence. Just drawing near to Him helps us to understand how the impossible things of life can turn into wonderful opportunities for Him to prove His faithfulness.

Things God Uses to Make a Difference

We cannot put God in a box. We can't say, "This is how He worked in the past, and I know He will follow the same route this time." Sometimes we greatly limit ourselves by watching for God to act in a certain way. He is faithful to His promises, but we cannot predict how He will work—only that He will if He has promised to do so.

God is very creative. He is infinite in knowledge while we are earthbound in our thoughts and reasoning. Most of us would not have chosen to save the man who would one day lead the nation of Israel out of bondage by placing him in a wicker basket and setting it adrift on the Nile River, only to be pulled from the water by Pharaoh's daughter. Moses grew up in the household of God's enemy! When people talk about the ways of God, they often want to pull out a theology book and point to sources that they believe contain great knowledge and insight. There is no doubt that the study of theology is important, but our quest for divine knowledge should begin with one primary source and that is God's Word, which is basic, straightforward, and directly applicable to our lives. God always works this way. A wicker basket covered with tar and pitch is nothing until you put something valuable in it. Then it becomes something of tremendous worth. Moses' life, for a season, was in a wicker basket. But that little ark was held, protected, and steered by the hand of almighty God. It could have drifted into the shipping lanes or floated along for days until Moses died, but that was never a possibility because God had a plan, and He was committed to protecting Moses until he had fulfilled the purpose of God.

Have you ever considered how valuable you are to God? You may think, *What can I do?* You can begin by never underestimating the things God uses. A wicker basket was just right for the first step in sending His deliverer deeper into Egypt where one day he would be used greatly by God.

One of the ways He works in our lives is to position us for future service. There are times when very young children want to walk forward to receive Christ at the end of one of our worship services. They may be five, six, or seven years old, and their actions may appear very unimportant to those who are anxious to leave. But in God's eyes, their lives are of utmost importance. He has a specific purpose in mind for them, and this is their first of many steps of obedience and blessings.

When we think about the things that God uses, one of the most striking stories in the Bible is that of Jonah. As children, some people may have heard his story about how he was swallowed by a very large fish. But there is more to this story than being in the belly of a whale. Jonah was a renegade preacher. God called him to do something, but he refused to answer His call:

> The word of the LORD came to Jonah the son of Amittai saying, "Arise, go to Nineveh the great city and cry against it, for their wickedness has come up before Me." But Jonah rose up to flee to Tarshish from the presence of the LORD. So he went down to Joppa, found a ship which was going to Tarshish, paid the fare and went down into it to go with them to Tarshish from the presence of the LORD. (Jonah 1:1–3)

Nineveh was the Assyrian capital city. It would now be a part of the city of Mosul, which is a major city in Iraq. Because the Ninevites were wicked, vicious warriors, they were very bloodthirsty, and they also were Israel's dire enemies. When Jonah heard that God wanted to send him to preach repentance to this nation, he decided that there was no way he was going to do it.

At some point, most of us have done what Jonah did—he ran in the opposite direction of obedience. Life turns stormy, and the clouds do not roll away. Disappointments come and linger. Anger builds, and the last thing we want to do is to forgive someone who has hurt us. God instructs us to do one thing, but we refuse to do it. Instead of trusting and obeying Him, we are tempted to do what seems best from our perspective. And at this point many people open the door to sin and rebellion. The urge to run away from difficulty and hardship becomes very strong.

Jonah wanted to escape his circumstance but not because he was afraid. The fact was that he was angry. He absolutely did not want Israel's enemies to receive mercy from God. He knew that if he preached repentance to the people of Nineveh, and they turned from their wickedness, God would spare their lives. But Jonah's desire for the people living in the city was death and destruction. Therefore, he ignored God's will and sovereignty. He caught a ride on the first ship leaving Joppa and headed for Tarshish, which, in ancient times, represented the absolute opposite end of the Levantine commercial trading sphere. In other words, there was no farther place that he could go. Sailing to Tarshish was like going to the ends of the known world.

As a prophet of God, he knew he could not escape His presence, but he ignored this and made a clear-cut decision not to preach God's message to the people of this very wicked city. Yet even though Jonah made a calculated decision to leave the scene, he was still in the crosshairs of God. As the psalmist wrote, "Even the darkness is not dark to You, and the night is as bright as the day. Darkness and light are alike to [God]" (Ps. 139:12). If you think there is a place where you can hide from God, you are dead wrong. It is absolutely foolish to believe that you can run from His presence. But this is exactly what many people do. They think that by refusing to go to church, they can run from Him. Or they believe that when they ignore His will for their lives, God will somehow forget what He has called them to do and change His mind. When people are disobedient, they suffer the consequences, just as Jonah did:

The LORD hurled a great wind on the sea and there was a great storm on the sea so that the ship was about to break up. Then the sailors became afraid and every man cried to his god, and they threw the cargo which was in the ship into the sea to lighten it for them. But Jonah had gone below into the hold of the ship, lain down and fallen sound asleep. So the captain approached him and said, "How is it that you are sleeping? Get up, call on your god. Perhaps your god will be concerned about us so that we will not perish." (Jonah 1:4–6)

Don't be deceived: sin affects everyone it touches. It hurts not only the person directly involved, but those who are close as well. Jonah's refusal to obey God placed the sailors in life-threatening peril. His self-centered actions almost cost the lives of all who were onboard the ship. Finally the men cast lots to see who was responsible for the calamity they were facing, and God allowed the lot to fall on Jonah (v. 7).

Can you imagine the scene as the sailors rushed belowdeck to retrieve the one who was responsible for such an all-consuming storm? As they pulled him up on deck, the prophet did not deny that what they were facing was a result of his being onboard. "I am a Hebrew," he said, "and I fear the LORD God of heaven who made the sea and the dry land" (v. 9). Notice what he did not tell them: "I'm God's servant. I've committed my life to His work, He has given me a task to do, and I have flat out refused." He never mentioned the fact that he was on the run from an omniscient God who had instructed him to go to a city in the opposite direction from where they were sailing. He was off course—not by a few miles but by many miles, and he was in serious trouble.

Jonah's job was to obey the Lord. God's will is not open for discussion. This is where many people fail to do what is right. They see a situation that does not fit the way they believe God operates, and they end up not doing what He wants them to do—thus, the reason for Jonah's rebellion. If God sends you in a certain direction, be assured that He has a plan. He wants you to arrive at His destination in time and not plot your own course, which will lead you to a place far from His will.

What to Do When You Know You Are Wrong

Jonah must have known his fate was sealed because he could not bear being above deck. Though the seas were violent and prayer was needed if all were to survive, he continued to act irresponsibly by falling asleep and ignoring the problem. This course of action never works. You can try dismissing a situation, but it will never get any better until you take the following steps:

Admit the Problem

I often talk with people who have allowed bitterness and unforgiveness to remain in their hearts for years. When I question them about this, they answer, "You don't know what she did to me. I'll never forgive her!" They truly believe—or I should say that they are totally committed to believing—that their actions are correct. God instructs us to forgive those who have hurt us, and that is for one reason: He does not want us to be captivated by anything other than His love. You may say, "I'm not held captive by him or her." But the truth is, you are.

Forgiveness does not mean that what the other person did was right. It means you forgive that person because God has commanded you to do this. He is completely able to deal with your offender, but as long as you are determined to hold a grudge and maintain your anger-laden defense, He will be hampered in His actions on your behalf. Yes, He can and will deal with the person who has hurt you. But His dealings may include the person's repentance and salvation. Jonah did not want this to happen to the Ninevites and his life ended in misery, but yours does not have to end the same way. God hears your prayers. He knows the hurt and frustration you feel. If you will ask for His help and understanding, He will lift your burden and free you from the bondage of resentment and bitterness.

Acknowledge God's Sovereignty

When you get to a point where you bow before a burning bush, you realize God is greater than you or anything you can do to help yourself. Sometimes people who have wealth and power usually have a very difficult time bowing to the Lord because they have the financial ability to rescue themselves. Others stiffen at the prospect of God's telling them what to do. I remember my shock when an older woman confessed to me that she had left her husband and moved to another part of the country. "He wanted to tell me what to do," she said. "And no one tells me what I should and should not do." For a moment I was speechless because I realized as we talked further that, her husband never abused her. He was a faithful provider, but she just did not want to be under his authority as a husband and the father of her children. Miles from home she was battling a serious illness and refused to acknowledge that God might be trying to get her attention.

We often fail to see the big picture, which is God's will and plan for our lives as believers. Instead, we fall for the trap that our feelings, likes, and dislikes are more important than doing what is right in God's eyes. This woman failed to realize that from the time we are born until the time we die, God places various authority figures in our lives. We may walk away from one situation, but if we have failed to do what is right and best from His perspective, we will face the same challenge all over again. This is how God works. He does not punish us or send discipline into our lives without a reason. When we act in rebellion, we can be certain that He will allow another problem to surface, which will address the same issue. I have urged people to respond correctly to God's discipline the first time an issue arises. You don't have to end up like Jonah. When you submit your hurts and hesitations to the Lord, He will take you step by step to a place in your heart where you can accept His will and grow through the experience in a way that will bring a multitude of blessings.

Ask God to Forgive Your Sin and Rebellion

The shortest route to forgiveness is the distance between your knees and the floor. God knows when you are being sincere and when you are just giving lip service to Him. I am convinced that those who refuse to release their disappointments and hurts to the Lord are not fully aware of God's sovereignty. If they were, they would not doubt His immense love for them, His desire to heal their hurts, and His promise to work out everything according to His purpose and plan. To refuse Him is to say no to the holy, omnipotent God who loves you with a love that is more powerful and resilient than anything this world has known or will know.

Pray for His Guidance

Jonah might have thought that he was a dead man. But it became clear that God's will would prevail. At first the pagan sailors with the prophet refused to throw him into the water. However, they soon realized that unless they did, all would perish. Their attempts to reach land failed, and they prayed, "We earnestly pray, O Lord, do not let us perish on account of this man's life and do not put innocent blood on us; for You, O Lord, have done as You have pleased" (Jonah 1:14). They picked up the prophet and threw him into the raging sea. Immediately the water became calm. Then they offered a sacrifice to the Lord.

I have known some people who have tried to run from God, and they ran right into a serious storm. More than likely, someone who is reading this book is running from God. Everywhere you turn the wind is blowing hard against you. The waves of stress are building, and you feel as though you are about to sink. Finally it is dawning on you that you cannot outrun God. The moment Jonah landed in the belly of the whale, he knew that he had only one choice to make, and it was obedience to God.

God used Jonah's disobedience to gain everyone's attention, including His wayward prophet. Suddenly everyone onboard that ship knew that God was in charge of the wind, rain, and ocean. After the sea grew calm, the sailors offered a sacrifice to the Lord for sparing their lives.

God narrowed Jonah's world to a point that the prophet had no choice other than to obey the Lord. God used the overwhelming situation to gain His prophet's attention. Jonah knew exactly why the weather had turned so stormy, and he also understood that there was only one way to quench the fury that was being displayed; that was through personal surrender. If you sense God shaking your life—trying to gain your attention—don't wait until you are in Jonah's position. Don't try God's patience and risk the outcome of disobedience. God's ways are deeply loving, but they are also powerful, purposeful, and unpredictable. You can't say, "God won't address this sin in my life." Yes, He will because He loves you too much to allow you to go to Tarshish and miss His blessing. Or He may just allow you to make half the journey, but like Jonah, you may end up in the belly of a very large fish.

God redirected the focus of Jonah's quest. "The LORD appointed a great fish to swallow Jonah, and Jonah was in the stomach of the fish three days and three nights" (Jonah 1:17). The prophet could not even die apart from God. In the tragic circumstances, God was in the process of directing his life, calling the shots, and getting his attention. And Jonah finally responded: "I called out of my distress to the LORD, and He answered me. I cried for help from the depth of Sheol; You heard my voice" (Jonah 2:1–2). After the prophet prayed, the next visual we gain from Scripture is the fish delivering him on dry land pointing in the direction of Nineveh.

God used Jonah to motivate a very wicked nation to seek God's forgiveness. Most of us know how this portion of the story ends. Jonah preached a revival message to the people living in this city, and the people turned from their wickedness. God accomplished His purpose, but Jonah remained bitter and angry. He finally did what God had called and trained him to do, but the last glimpse of his life that we are given in Scripture is dismal. He was angry that God had relented and not destroyed the city:

> It greatly displeased Jonah. . . . He prayed to the LORD and said, "Please LORD, was not this what I said while I was still in my own country? Therefore in order to forestall this I fled to Tarshish, for I knew that You are a gracious and compassionate God, slow to anger and abundant in loving-kindness, and one who relents concerning calamity. Therefore now, O LORD, please take my life from me, for death is better to me than life." (Jonah 4:1–3)

Jonah didn't get it! He never understood that God's way in this matter was not his way. Begrudgingly he obeyed God and then was furious when the Lord did not come to the same conclusion as the one he believed to be right. There was no hint of joy in doing what God had trained him to do. While the Lord achieved His purpose, Jonah came up the loser.

No Limit to God's Ability

What is God's goal for our lives? He certainly does not want us to turn in the direction of Tarshish. He wants us to have a desire to obey Him but not because we know we must or the bottom of life will drop out from beneath us. That is not how God wants us to view our lives with Him. He loves us and wants us to desire something better, and that is to understand His ways. If Jonah had moved past his feelings of anger and bitterness, he probably would have adopted a different perspective—one that proclaimed, "God, while I don't understand why You would want me to preach repentance to our enemies, I will. Instead of praying for their destruction, I'll pray that they come to know You as God of the universe because I know Your ways are not my ways. In the end, I believe You will vindicate Your people." We can't become entangled in "why, God?" We must trust Him and know that He is working regardless of what we can see.

In this case, God used a mighty fish to turn Jonah around. He used a burning bush to gain Moses' attention. And we can think of other examples of the things God used in the lives of those recorded in His Word. David walked down to a stream and chose five smooth stones, placed them in a pouch at his side, and walked back to a battlefield where he met Goliath (1 Sam. 17:40). King Saul had tried to persuade him to wear his kingly armor, but David's heart was set on gaining the victory the way that God had trained him—by using elements so ridiculously simple that those who had gathered for the battle would be tempted to laugh at him. Can you grasp the wisdom of God at work in these events? He is the only One who is to receive glory. Moses was God's chosen deliverer, but only the Lord could work the miracles needed to free the nation. David was the anointed king of Israel, but it was God who ruled his heart and won the victory the day he fought the Philistine giant.

What is the one thing God is using in your life to gain a great triumph? His ways are not limited to things that appear successful on the surface. He can use even failure if you will submit your life to Him and allow Him to bring restitution. That was what He wanted to do in Jonah's life. And that was what He did in Peter's life. Though he had been with Jesus three years, there was still a sense of cockiness within his life. God used his denial of Christ at the most crucial of times to wean him of his embedded pride (Luke 22:34). After the resurrection, Jesus restored him and commissioned him along with the other disciples to carry His word of hope and truth to a lost world. There is no limit to what God can do when you give Him free access to your life.

Does God change everyone? Does He save every person? No. This is His desire, but some people refuse to allow Him to work in their lives. Or if they drop their guards, it is only to a certain level and not fully. You and I must recognize that God uses all kinds of things to get our attention and ultimately to accomplish His will. A wicker basket saved Moses. A stone in David's hand became a weapon that led to a mighty victory. Achieving a mighty victory for God could have happened in Jonah's life. And while the people of Nineveh responded to God's call of repentance, His prophet ended up sulking in anger. He missed a divine opportunity—something that does not happen every day. He also failed to experience the joy that comes from obeying the Lord.

Too many people today live in a storm because they are running from God. They think that if they drink enough, take enough drugs, have enough money, or have enough relationships, somehow they will be able to silence the howling winds and calm the raging waves of fear—but they cannot. Why do so many people want to commit suicide? They come to the end of themselves, the end of their abilities, and the end of life, and they still refuse to pray for God's help. They are in total despair. They see no hope. But I want to assure everyone reading these words that there is hope. If you are willing to listen to the voice of God and willing to respond to His call, He will use something to gain your attention, take you to a deeper level of love and devotion to Him, and in the process transform the lives of those around you. Peter's commitment did not stall in the face of defeat: it deepened. God sifted and refined him to such a degree that he became the bearer of His truth to everyone he met. The Lord's purpose is always for the good, not only for you but for someone else, too.

When I think about His ability to use things that most of us would discount, I'm reminded of how Jesus fed five thousand people with a young boy's lunch:

> After these things Jesus went away to the other side of the Sea of Galilee (or Tiberias). A large crowd followed Him, because they saw the signs which He was performing on those who were sick. Then Jesus went up on

the mountain, and there He sat down with His disciples. Now the Passover, the feast of the Jews, was near. Therefore Jesus, lifting up His eyes and seeing that a large crowd was coming to Him, said to Philip, "Where are we to buy bread, so that these may eat?" This He was saying to test him, for He Himself knew what He was intending to do. Philip answered Him, "Two hundred denarii worth of bread is not sufficient for them, for everyone to receive a little." One of His disciples, Andrew, Simon Peter's brother, said to Him, "There is a lad here who has five barley loaves and two fish, but what are these for so many people?" (John 6:1–9)

God is not limited by circumstances. Sometimes you think He cannot use you. He used a stone, a slingshot, a big fish, a basket, and a bush, and He certainly can use you. This young boy probably had come with his family to hear the Savior, and he ended up being in the right place at the right time to be used by the Lord in a miraculous way. Jesus wanted to drive home the fact that He was God's Son and our only source of provision and strength.

Many people miss great opportunities because they feel that what they have to offer is not very much. Or perhaps something in their past is a point of personal shame and embarrassment. Others may think that what God is asking them to do does not fit their hopes and plans for the future. So, they allow the opportunity to come and go without accepting His offer. In His quest to know God, Moses failed horribly. He ended up murdering an Egyptian and being banished to the wilderness for forty years. But when God knew Moses was ready to accept His challenge, He spoke to Moses from the fire of the burning bush.

All this lad had to offer was two fish and five barley loaves of bread. Yet it was more than enough in the hands of Jesus:

Jesus said, "Have the people sit down." . . . [He] then took the loaves, and having given thanks, He distributed to those who were seated; likewise also of the fish as much as they wanted. When they were filled, He said to His disciples, "Gather up the leftover fragments so that nothing will be lost." So they gathered them up, and filled twelve baskets with fragments from the five barley loaves which were left over by those who had eaten. Therefore when the people saw the sign which He had performed, they said, "This is truly the Prophet who is to come into the world." (John 6:10–14)

Often God's miracles are given in such a way that they meet very important needs. But one thing is certain: they always are used to draw people to Himself. We would never think of trying to divide several loaves of bread to feed thousands of people, but Jesus did because He is Lord over all things and He is the Bread of Life. In order for their hunger to be satisfied, the people only needed to taste what He was offering them.

The Fallout from Saying No to God

You can live forty, fifty years or more and then all of a sudden look back and think, *God, I didn't know that was what You wanted to do.* We cannot see the future results of our obedience. We may imagine what God could do, but we do not have a way of knowing for sure how He will use the things we offer Him. Suppose this young boy had said no and run off into the crowd. You might think, *Well, he would have had another opportunity.* That may be true, but it would not be like the one Jesus offered at that moment. For the rest of his life, that young man remembered what it was like to be in the Savior's presence as he handed Him his small but very significant lunch.

Another example of extreme faith and obedience is the widow mentioned in Mark 12:41–44. When she placed two small coins in the offertory, Jesus told His disciples, "Truly I say to you, this poor widow put in more than all the contributors to the treasury; for they all put in out of their surplus, but she, out of her poverty, put in all she owned, all she had to live on." When you and I are fully surrendered to God, we give everything to Him. Whatever He chooses to use is up to Him. But I want you to understand that often He uses the simplest, most ordinary things to bring about the greatest results. The amount this woman gave was less than a penny, but that was unimportant. Her obedience and her devotion to God, however, were important. The issue was attitude. Are we just giving a portion of ourselves to God, or do we give Him everything? This was not a tip that this woman placed in the collection box. It was much more because it was given not out of a surplus but out of poverty. The world looks at people who are very wealthy and seeks to elevate them. But God ignores the very things that appear to be so popular with society.

I could probably list many things that you would like to hold on to and not relinquish to the Lord: money, a relationship, a desire, or a social position. Often people will give to God's work because they think that it will ease their guilt. They may sacrifice in other ways and even feel compelled to do more to help those who have less than they have. The things they should refuse to give up are the ones they relinquish far too easily—prayer, worship, service, and friendship to God. They want to believe that at the end of their lives, somehow the good they have done will outweigh any wrong they have been involved with over their lifetimes. He does forgive when we confess our sins, but we are the ones who lose so very much.

Several things happen when we refuse to surrender ourselves to God:

We miss His blessings. If I asked you whether you would want to have God's blessings—the things that He sends your way that are bountiful and beyond anything you can imagine or what you could do for yourself—I know what your answer would be. No one in his right mind would say, "I'll take what I can do on my own apart from the omnipotent, sovereign God." But countless people do just that. They say, "No thanks, Lord," and go on to live very narrow and restrictive lives even though their journeys and travels may take them around the world. Solomon asked, "What is the advantage to him who toils for the wind? Throughout his life he also eats in darkness with great vexation, sickness and anger" (Eccl. 5:16–17). In other words, what is the purpose of living and gaining so much apart from God? His ways are not a mystery to those who live according to His principles. You may not know all there is to know, but the things you will know and experience are peace, joy, love, happiness, contentment, fellowship, and eternal life. You can have all that you can gather and acquire, or you can have what God gives, which is always so much more.

We miss His fellowship. Years ago I counseled a man who had been in an adulterous affair. His wife had forgiven him, but he could not forgive himself. This feeling created a distance between him and her that prevented them from enjoying each other's fellowship. They were together and even laughed and talked, but there was a wall separating them. The more the husband struggled with what he had done, the more the enemy tried to convince him that there was a chance that he would repeat the same offense. His relationship with God suffered because he felt guilty.

It took a great deal of time, but finally he surrendered to the truth that, regardless of what he had done, God loved him. He began really opening up to the love of God. He prayed in the morning before going to work, and during the day he purposefully stopped to consider God's goodness toward him. One day he called my office excited and just wanted to tell me that everything was going to be okay because he had discovered that God had not stopped loving him. And he could risk loving his wife because of the relationship he had established with the Lord.

Our relationship with Jesus Christ affects our relationships with others. If we feel cold or reserved toward God, we will feel the same toward those we love. In this case, restoration and godly truth were the key factors in bringing emotional healing and victory over Satan's wicked scheme. Many of us grew up singing the chorus of "Just As I Am":

Just as I am, without one plea,
But that Thy blood was shed for me,
And that Thou bidd'st me come to Thee,
O Lamb of God, I come! I come!

The simple truth is this: when you come to God, He opens up His arms and gathers you into Himself. You don't have to be or do anything more than you are right now. And you may know Him as your Savior, but you have fought, like Jonah, against doing what you know He has called you to do. His way is simple: "Obey Me and watch Me work in your life. Or resist Me and experience what life feels like living on the run to Tarshish."

We miss the incredible experience of being caught up in His intimate love and care. As long as we are standing at a distance—not fully surrendered to God—we are the ones who lose. We miss the most awesome opportunity that we will ever have, and that is to be personally, unconditionally loved by God. Nothing compares to this. If our minds are full of other things and we are not serious about our relationship with Him, we will not learn how to be secure and "at home" with the God of the universe. People search endlessly for ways to feel that they are truly loved. They become involved in relationships that are anything but godly and wonder why they feel lonely and forgotten.

The one Person who has promised never to forget you is standing right beside you. Don't turn away from His love. Let Him embrace you and care for you. I can promise you this: if you do, you will never feel lonely again. There may be times you are alone, but when the love of God burns in your heart, you will be able to face anything and know that He is holding your hand.

God made a choice for His Son to die on a cross, which was probably hand hewed from the wood of a very common tree. Why do you think He wanted Jesus to be nailed to a tree? Recently I thought about this and wondered, *Who cut that tree down? How old was it? How long did it stand, and where was it located?* God knew every answer to these questions. He led the cutter to cut it down, trim it, and shape it. It was probably a Roman citizen who worked on the cross that would crucify the Son of God. After it was assembled, it was probably stacked in a pile of others waiting for that crucial moment when it would bear the weight of the Savior of the world.

Placing Jesus on a cross positioned Him to be seen by everyone who was present. There was no question about His crucifixion. It happened just as the prophets foretold. There was one tree, with one set of hands shaping the wood—cutting it, carving it, and preparing it. From our perspective, it was being prepared for a horrendous deed; but from God's viewpoint, it was exactly what He planned. Jesus came to earth to die for our sins. He paid the sin-debt of the world so that any- and everyone who comes to Him would experience unconditional forgiveness, love, and eternal life. It was not just *a* tree. It was *the* tree.

What can God do in your life if you are willing to sing the following chorus?

> *All to Jesus I surrender, all to Him I freely give;*
> *I will ever love and trust Him, in His presence daily live.*

The answer is more than you can imagine and much more than anything you can gain on your own apart from Him. There is only one way to discover His best, and it begins the moment you surrender all.

Chapter Five

GOD BRINGS GOOD
FROM EVIL

The woman on the telephone sounded more than just frustrated. She sounded disheartened—a feeling that each one of us has known at some point. She had been through a series of personal losses and trials that had left her feeling exhausted mentally and emotionally. I listened intently as she painfully explained the latest development. Then I offered the same advice that had worked for me whenever I was facing trouble on all fronts. I advised her to be still before the Lord, to seek His wisdom—and no matter how tempted she may be to turn to her own devices, to surrender every thought and desire of personal effort to Him in prayer. In other words: "Be still, and know that [He is] God" (Ps. 46:10 NIV). The New American Standard Bible has it this way: "Cease striving and know that I am God." In Psalm 37, David wrote this about resting in the Lord:

> Rest in the LORD and wait patiently for Him;
> Do not fret because of him who prospers in his way,
> Because of the man who carries out wicked schemes.

Cease from anger and forsake wrath;

Do not fret; it leads only to evildoing.

For evildoers will be cut off,

But those who wait for the LORD, they will inherit the land.

Yet a little while and the wicked man will be no more;

And you will look carefully for his place and he will not be there. (vv. 7–10)

At times, God's ways can seem perplexing. One reason is our lack of understanding of the way He works. Another reason is our desire to be set free quickly from trouble, heartache, or disappointment. The fact is, no one enjoys hardship and difficulty. We may accept the challenge when trouble first appears, but after a season or two we are ready to be freed of our emotional, physical, or mental pain. The enemy tempts us into thinking that God really is *not* doing the best thing in our lives, and we end up questioning His wisdom.

The woman that I mentioned above concluded our conversation with a very interesting thought. She said, "I guess I just don't know how God operates." I assured her that there is a way to know God—how He thinks, works, and responds to our needs. We can know His ways, but we must be committed to knowing Him—intimately and personally. This means opening up His Word and asking Him to give us a desire to read what He has written. No matter how great the tragedy or the problem, always remember God's love is deeper, and He always has a fantastic purpose in mind for every trial we face.

One of the ways He operates is to use the wicked to accomplish His plan in our lives. Most of us know the story of Joseph by heart. On the surface, there is probably very little I could discuss that would seem new and revealing. But instead of looking at his situation from the perspectives of what he did or did not do, I want to examine what God allowed to happen and why He acted the way He did.

Entangled and Trapped

Maybe you feel like you are facing one problem after another. It seems as if the more you pray and the greater your commitment, the more life unravels. If you could, you would grab a needle and a spool of strong thread and sew it up. But that is not what God has provided. There are no shortcuts around suffering. There is no easy way through the trouble God asks you to face. You may come to a point where you think the only thing you seem to have is your faith in God. If this is the case, I want to assure you that it is more than enough.

Joseph's brothers despised him. Their jealousy and envy ran so deep that they conspired to kill him (Gen. 37:18). There will be times when life is not easy. Some of our greatest emotional injuries come at the hands of those we love and thought we knew. But just as we have God's promises to fall upon in times of discouragement, we also have His keen insight into the heartache we will face.

In fact, David wrote,

> Give ear to my prayer, O God;
> And do not hide Yourself from my supplication.
> Give heed to me and answer me;
> I am restless in my complaint and am surely distracted,
> Because of the voice of the enemy,
> Because of the pressure of the wicked;
> For they bring down trouble upon me
> And in anger they bear a grudge against me.
> My heart is in anguish within me,
> And the terrors of death have fallen upon me.
> Fear and trembling come upon me,
> And horror has overwhelmed me.

I said, "Oh, that I had wings like a dove!

I would fly away and be at rest.". . .

For it is not an enemy who reproaches me,

Then I could bear it;

Nor is it one who hates me who has exalted himself against me,

Then I could hide myself from him.

But it is you, a man my equal,

My companion and my familiar friend. (Ps. 55:1–6, 12–13)

David's conclusion to his dire circumstances should rally our hearts to trust God all the more, even when we do not understand why severe trials have come our way: "Cast your burden upon the LORD and He will sustain you; He will never allow the righteous to be shaken" (v. 22).

God can and will use wicked circumstances to accomplish His purpose. You may think, *There is no way this can happen. I have experienced tragedy and a very deep hurt. I'm not sure that I can even trust God.* From a human perspective, Joseph may have been tempted to agree, but once he turned his heart toward the Lord, there was no question. He knew his only option was to trust God.

Nothing escapes His attention, especially the events and circumstances that touch your life. Just as He was aware of Joseph's every need, He is aware of yours. He knows and understands. He never dismisses or overlooks unrighteous, wicked, and evil deeds. You may wonder where He is and why He did not show up when you needed Him the most. The truth is, He never leaves. There is never a time when He logs out of your life or takes a break. He is always aware of what is taking place and He wants you to know that He is 100 percent on your team. He created you and He knows the plan that He has for your future. You may have adversity, but you can be assured that you will also experience times of extreme blessing as you grow in awareness of His ways, love, and plans. I'm sure Joseph wondered how he ended up at what appeared to be a dead end. God had given him awesome insight into the future: one day he would reign over his brothers (Gen. 37:1–11). But in the beginning, his unbridled boldness, coupled with the fact that his father, Jacob, loved him deeply, only fueled his brothers' jealousy to a point where they reacted in wickedness.

God allowed Joseph to deal with the challenges that came from being betrayed by members of his own family. For you, betrayal may come through a good friend or a coworker. Rather than kill him, Joseph's brothers decided to throw him in a pit that had been dug to capture wild animals. They walked away without a tug to their consciences. Only Reuben returned to the pit and saw that Joseph was gone (Gen. 37:29). His change of heart came too late, however. A band of Midianite merchants had pulled Joseph out of the pit. But their intentions were equally wicked, and they sold him into slavery to a group of Ishmaelites for twenty shekels of silver. These men took him to Egypt where he was purchased by Potiphar, an Egyptian officer of Pharaoh (Gen. 37:28; 39:1).

Without them knowing it, the Lord used Joseph's brothers to begin the process of Israel's future deliverance from bondage. Though years away, God's ultimate goal was to lay a foundation for their future redemption. Joseph's suffering was a staging point for the deliverance of God's people— not just Israel—but of all men and women. When you are trying to discern God's ways, always maintain a perspective that has the future in mind. Shortsightedness will tempt you to believe that you must have an answer to your problem *right now*. But having a desire to see your circumstances from God's viewpoint changes the way you respond to the situation and to others.

God Uses Tragedy

Have you ever wondered while standing at a loved one's graveside how anything good could come of his or her death? In some cases, it is easy to understand what God is doing, but others are more difficult. Recently a friend told me about a funeral she attended. The older woman who died had been a Christian for many years. Yet this faithful saint spent the last year of her life fighting a losing battle with cancer. As her children gathered for her memorial service, several expressed doubts about God's sovereignty in allowing their mother to suffer. In their younger years, she had been a pillar of strength to the family following the untimely death of their father. Why would God allow such a dreaded disease to strike and claim her life? It did not seem right from their perspective. But this godly woman understood something more about the Lord than they did.

When she felt well enough to visit with her pastor, she told him exactly what she wanted her funeral to be like—not expressing sadness or even the slightest hint of defeat. "When everyone here is crying," she mused, "I'll be rejoicing and praising God!" She went on to explain that she knew several in her family did not know the Savior. They had never prayed to receive Him as Lord of their lives. Now, she was just about to see Him face-to-face, and her dying wish was that each one would come to know the joy of having a personal relationship with Jesus Christ. And this is exactly what happened. At the close of the funeral service, the pastor asked those present who wanted to accept Christ as Savior. Several family members raised their hands.

God uses tragedy—even wicked events—to accomplish His purposes. Joseph was thrown into a pit used to trap wild animals. Later, he was sold as a slave in Egypt, but the trials did not stop there. Potiphar's wife tried to seduce him, and when he did not accept her offer, she lied about the incident and he was thrown into jail. Imagine what went through his mind. God had preserved his life and had even blessed him, though he was held captive in a foreign land. Potiphar had appointed him head of his household. Joseph had power, a certain amount of security, and even a position, but all of that dissolved very quickly when the Lord allowed a wicked person to attack his character.

Most of us would have been on our knees asking *why*, but we really do not see Joseph doing that in Scripture. We can imagine that he wondered what was going on, but the one thing that comes through in this story of faith under trial is Joseph's desire to remain steadfast and not sin against God. He wasn't in jail long before the jailer realized that he was a very gifted young man and made him the overseer of the jail: "The LORD was with Joseph and extended kindness to him, and gave him favor in the sight of the chief jailer. The chief jailer committed to Joseph's charge all the prisoners who were in the jail; so that whatever was done there, he was responsible for it" (Gen. 39:21–22). From a human perspective, it appeared that any hope Joseph had for a future was over. But I want to challenge you never to calculate a situation without adding in the faithfulness of God.

How could any good come from this evil situation? When God is involved, there is always a way. He was positioning Joseph for a greater purpose. The evil that was done to him was part of God's omniscient plan. He did not leave Joseph in prison forever. Yet before his release, the Lord allowed him to experience even more betrayal. This time, another inmate promised to work on Joseph's behalf once he was released. But that did not happen, and Joseph spent more time confined in a place that he never should have been forced to enter.

Think about this: Pharaoh never would have considered him for the position of prime minister. No leader of Egypt would have embraced the idea of a Hebrew boy joining his cabinet. But once Joseph was securely in the country without any hope of escaping to his father, God could begin to work. In time, Joseph's ability to interpret dreams was uncovered, and he had the perfect opportunity to use his gift in the presence of Pharaoh himself. The result was not just Joseph's release from jail, but his release and his promotion to administrator over all of Egypt. He went from the dungeon to the palace with no self-promotional stops in between. It was solely the result of God's awesome work in his life. And right on time, a famine swept throughout the land and hit Israel especially hard.

We know the end of the story. Joseph saved his family, and ultimately God's people, from a sure death. Because he was the prime minister and because he was in charge of the country's granaries, he knew Egypt had a surplus. Once he and his brothers were reunited, Joseph moved his family to safety in the foreign country (Gen. 42–46). The Lord used every unbelieving, wicked person to accomplish His goal. Every event, heartache, betrayal, burden, and moment spent in loneliness had purpose.

Years later, the present Pharaoh began to think about the Israelites and the power they held by their sheer numbers. Israel's twelve sons were no longer a small family. Their family membership had grown to the thousands.

Joseph died, and all his brothers and all that generation. But the sons of Israel were fruitful and increased greatly, and multiplied, and became exceedingly mighty, so that the land was filled with them. Now a new king arose over Egypt, who did not know Joseph. He said to his people, "Behold, the people of the sons of Israel are more and mightier than we. Come, let us deal wisely with them, or else they will multiply and in the event of war, they will also join themselves to those who hate us, and fight against us and depart from the land." So they appointed taskmasters over them to afflict them with hard labor. (Ex. 1:6–11)

Most of us know the account of this story by heart, but let's take a different look into what I believe God was doing in the life of the nation. It is the same thing He wants to do in our lives.

The Disadvantage of Seeing Life from a Human Perspective

We always need to remember that God's ways are *not* ours. Many times, the course we would choose to travel is not what He plans. Therefore, we see

His work and fail to understand what He is doing. Or if the process becomes too painful, we want to bolt and look for the first open door away from the hurt. Our hearts are breaking, our lives feel shattered, and we feel as though the sun will never shine again, but we continue to fight against God's will.

We cannot fully understand the way He thinks. We have limited abilities. God, however, is infinite in nature. Difficulty comes, and the first thing most people do is wonder, *Lord, where did I go wrong?* It lingers, and we become convinced that we are to blame—even though this usually is not the case. God does not assign blame in the way we do. He knows when we have made a critical mistake, and He deals with us at that point. But often when we experience the wickedness of this world that ignites feelings of stress and untold pressure, it is because we have run up against the evil forces of a fallen world.

Young people like to say, "Get over it," when faced with a situation that makes little sense. In a way, we also need to "get over" our frantic desire to live in a perfect world while we are on this earth. It is not going to happen, and we must "get past" our fears and begin to live in the infinite light and awesome hope that are ours through Jesus Christ. We are not defeated because His resurrection power lives within us. Nothing is greater, offers a brighter future, and has more potential than this. The world is passing away, but God is right where He said He would be—with you in every step you take.

We fail to see His ultimate goal, which is always for the best. We can be blinded by our dreams for the future or by what we think should be true or happen. I have watched many people become tripped up at this point. They believe their way is best, and even though God sends help and guidance, they remain committed to their course and often end up taking detours or missing His best altogether. Instead of being committed to advancement, be committed first to being in the middle of His will, and then you will know what true peace and joy feel like. And remember, joy, peace, and blessing do not always come in a material form—owning a large house, living in the "right" neighborhood, driving a new car, and having a high-level job. They come when we live our lives in step with His purposes and plans. Nothing brings more personal reward than being right where God wants you to be.

We can't always discern His purpose. Although we may not know what God is thinking, we can learn to be still and watch and listen for His guidance. He tells us that if we will seek Him, He will speak to us: "I will instruct you and teach you in the way you should go; I will counsel you and watch over you" (Ps. 32:8 NIV). He does this through prayer, through the study of His Word, and through those who minister to us. Always make sure that as you listen, you also ask God to give you His discernment so you will know when to move forward, when to wait, and when to rest in His care.

We need to pray, but we are too caught up in our desires, needs, feelings, and pressures. Satan will stop at nothing to distract us and keep us from seeing God's power in, through, and surrounding our lives. He whispers false accusations to our minds and hearts, and when we don't respond by becoming fearful and discouraged, he turns his attacks up another notch by telling us that others feel we are incompetent, insensitive, out of touch, and any number of wrong accusations. Don't fall for his weak threats and miserable lies. God has chosen you for a purpose. He saved you based on His unconditional love for you, and He has a plan for your life (Jer. 29:11). He has set His seal of ownership on your life (2 Cor. 1:21–22). You belong to Him, and the God of the universe, whose every thought is aimed in your direction, intimately loves you.

God Never Changes; He Is the God of Love

There are no exceptions to God's principles, but there certainly are times when He knows that the trial we are facing is far too great for us to handle.

It is perfectly normal and even reasonable to ask how He can use something as horrible as abuse or rape or some other perverse act in our lives. How can we ever think of living life to the fullest when we cannot see past the hurt we feel? *First*, we need to realize that God is not the author of evil. That role belongs strictly to Satan. He is the one who wants us to suffer. But we are not left alone to battle his wickedness. *Second*, we need to know that God Himself is our refuge and defense. The psalmist declared,

> God is our refuge and strength,
>
> A very present help in trouble.
>
> Therefore we will not fear, though the earth should change
>
> And though the mountains slip into the heart of the sea;
>
> Though its waters roar and foam,
>
> Though the mountains quake at its swelling pride.
>
> There is a river whose streams make glad the city of God,
>
> The holy dwelling places of the Most High.
>
> God is in the midst of her, she will not be moved;
>
> God will help her when morning dawns. (Ps. 46:1–5)

God is steadfast and faithful. There are some things we see that make little sense. Some things—especially sinister and evil events—will never make complete sense to us. David helps us gain crucial insight into this issue by writing,

> The wicked plots against the righteous
>
> And gnashes at him with his teeth.
>
> The Lord laughs at him,
>
> For He sees his day is coming.
>
> The wicked have drawn the sword and bent their bow
>
> To cast down the afflicted and the needy,

> To slay those who are upright in conduct.
>
> Their sword will enter their own heart,
>
> And their bows will be broken. (Ps. 37:12–15)

And in Psalm 34 we read,

> The eyes of the LORD are toward the righteous
>
> And His ears are open to their cry.
>
> The face of the LORD is against evildoers,
>
> To cut off the memory of them from the earth.
>
> The righteous cry, and the LORD hears
>
> And delivers them out of all their troubles.
>
> The LORD is near to the brokenhearted
>
> And saves those who are crushed in spirit.
>
> Many are the afflictions of the righteous,
>
> But the LORD delivers him out of them all. (vv. 15–19)

When we are faced with evil of any kind, the Lord is our strong tower, our immovable rock, and our deliverer (Ps. 18).

God had purposefully positioned Joseph in a place where years later the people would be delivered from bondage. Nothing is coincidental. God is involved in or aware of every event that takes place. We live in a fallen world. He doesn't plan evil, but He will use its harsh results to shape our lives and hearts so that they become reflections of His mercy.

Every time we disobey God, the wheels of judgment begin to turn. He had given the people of Israel two warnings: do not worship other gods, and do not intermarry (Deut. 7). Why was He concerned about their marriage partners? Because He knew that if they married people from pagan cultures, they would be tempted to worship pagan gods. Idol worship of any kind totally goes against God's commandments. Taking it into your home and family will dilute your love for God and tempt you to question His authority and relevance. It happens on the spiritual level, and it changes a person from the inside out.

Much of the evil in our world today is the result of one godless decision after another. God says, "That is detestable to Me; don't do it." And we compromise our actions or seek to justify what we are doing by telling ourselves that it is really not that bad, no one will get hurt, or everyone else is doing it. The question I often raise is this: "If everyone else is doing it and their lives are so miserable and broken, do you want to do the same thing?" Once I posed this question to a young man who was just about to make a horrendous mistake in a relationship. He was committed to taking a step that I knew would lead to deep sorrow and frustration. He quickly countered, "Most of my friends are doing it, and all of us are happy."

"Give it a few months and see if their happiness remains," I responded, and he did. In fact, several months passed, and one day I noticed that he was in church after being absent for a while. I quickly remembered our conversation. After the service, he walked up to me and took my hand and whispered, "I'm tired. I want to come back." No pastor enjoys seeing people suffer because of sin. And you want to respond the way God responds, which is always in love.

After his sin with Bathsheba, King David prayed,

> Against You, You only, I have sinned
> And done what is evil in Your sight,
> So that You are justified when You speak
> And blameless when You judge. . . .
> Create in me a clean heart, O God,
> And renew a steadfast spirit within me.
> Do not cast me away from Your presence
> And do not take Your Holy Spirit from me.

> Restore to me the joy of Your salvation
> And sustain me with a willing spirit.
> Then I will teach transgressors Your ways,
> And sinners will be converted to You. (Ps. 51:4, 10–13)

Do you understand what David did? He confessed that what he had done was wrong. He was aware of God's judgment about his sin, but he understood the Lord's intimate love for him. He prayed not only for God to forgive him but also for restoration so that he could be used to caution others not to disobey Him.

The Pathway of Failure

Another aspect of Israel's sin is its progression. From the very beginning, the hearts of the people were bent away from God. He delivered them, but they were not satisfied to have Him as their King. The political structure of pagan nations caught their attention, and they began to pressure the Lord to give them a king to rule over them. They had the King of kings to guide and protect them, but they wanted an earthly leader to govern them. I'm amazed when I hear people say that God's love is restrictive. I immediately think, *You don't know the love of God—the intimate, boundless, sacrificial love of almighty God. If you did, the words* restrictive *and* limiting *would never come to mind.* The only thing that restricted God from pouring out His love and blessings in abundance was Israel's disobedience.

The same thing restricts His work in our lives today. He wants to bless us, but our sinfulness prevents Him from doing this. Yet even here—in times of vile and wicked behavior—God is at work bringing men and women to a point of repentance. His ultimate purpose for the nation of Israel was to be a channel through which the Messiah would come. However, His immediate purpose for the people was to teach them to love and honor Him above all else. His promise to Abraham never lost its appeal. He said, "I will make you exceedingly fruitful, and I will make nations of you, and kings will come forth from you. I will establish My covenant between Me and you and your descendants after you throughout their generations for an everlasting covenant, to be God to you and to your descendants after you" (Gen. 17:6–7).

God always keeps His word. When He makes a promise, He fulfills it in His timing and in His way. By the time Israel left Egypt and began the journey to the promised land, the people did not remember who Abraham was. They had heard of him, but there was no personal identification. Through Moses, the Lord began to train and shape them into being the nation of "the promise." Today we are the people of promise, but we need to realize that our journey has a purpose. And even the failure that we encounter can be used to change and motivate us to desire His will over our own. Living the Christian life literally requires a shift in attitude where we come to a point of realization about who God is—He is sovereign and over all things. He also loves us with an everlasting love and has an amazing plan for our lives.

A few years ago, I thought of this in a fresh new way. I was on a photography trip in the northwest, and an unexpected snowstorm threatened travel to the places I wanted to visit. Many times we can plan exactly how we want something to unfold and have it turn out differently. I continue to enjoy the preparation process even before I leave for my destination. Laying out my clothes, packing my photography equipment, and spending time looking at maps of the area that I will visit always lift the level of my excitement. Now, I can go online and look up all the information I need about a given location. I also can imagine what it will be like to be there and take photographs.

On this trip, nothing in my planning could have prepared me for what I encountered. Once I arrived at my destination there was a dramatic shift in weather. It began to snow heavily. "Okay, Lord," I remember saying, "You must have something else in mind." I asked Him to show me the best route to take the next morning. When the snow did not let up, I felt tempted, as many people do, to wonder whether I had made a wrong decision by coming to this part of the country at this time of the year. As I watched weather reports and double-checked the latest news, I kept sensing Him say, *Trust Me*. God is even interested in small events like vacations that suddenly seem to come to a dead end.

Each time the thought of trusting Him entered my thoughts, I felt encouraged. Each time I turned on the television and saw the massive storm sitting over what seemed to be my cabin, I felt the opposite—discouraged. "Even if the sun comes out," I reasoned, "I will never be able to navigate through several feet of new snow." I was wrong. By the next morning, the sky was blue, and while not all the roads were passable, the ones that led to beautiful vistas were. But there was something more. Because of the snow storm, I saw my surroundings differently. It was not necessary to drive a great distance in order to witness the wonder of God's creation. Freshly fallen snow had left the surrounding forest encased in beauty so great that all that I saw and photographed amazed me.

You may be wondering how you ended up where you are. Godly men and women have wondered the same thing. The weight of the nation of Israel's future fell on Esther's shoulders. Joseph left his home one morning to meet up with his brothers, but he never came home again. Hannah prayed for a son promising to dedicate him to the Lord's service. Moses lifted up his eyes and saw a burning bush and found that his future had been instantly changed. David came in from the sheep field and was anointed the future king of Israel. One morning Peter, James, and John pulled their boats up on the shore and began cleaning their nets. A few minutes later, Jesus stopped to talk with them, and they left everything to follow Him. The journey into understanding God's ways is necessary. Each one of the men and women that God used faced many challenges. Trouble, disease, disappointment, failure, deep sorrow, and even death shadowed their every step. Many were misunderstood, but none of this altered what God had planned for them to do before the beginning of time. For us to understand how He works, we must accept the fact that life's pressures and tragedies play a very important part in our spiritual development.

Therefore, God uses trying circumstances and even wicked events and people to develop an awesome testimony within our lives. Soon, Israel's enemies began to know that Israel worshiped God and He was great. Pharaoh encountered His power firsthand as his armies were washed away in the Red Sea. Was God in this? Absolutely. He was in every single aspect of it. We would think that the people of Israel would never drift in their devotion to God, but they did. Again and again the Lord had to remind them of His greatness. And time after time, they had to endure serious losses and setbacks. Their love for God was diluted by a love for the world's passions and the gods of their enemies. As a result of their sin, the nation was weakened by compromise.

We are following the same path. Our political leaders have moved to take the Bible out of our schools, stop our children from praying, and recognize homosexuality as an acceptable lifestyle. Our young people believe that living together before marriage is perfectly normal and acceptable. A spirit of disrespect for the principles of God has drifted into our society. I have a friend who is a psychologist, and he tells me that he is seeing more emotional problems than ever. We always pay the price for wrong decisions. The tragedy is this: everyone gets hurt in the process. You cannot change the laws of God. You cannot alter His principles. If we forget history, we will be destined to repeat it. Israel spent forty years in the wilderness before they entered the promised land. Once they were there, they failed to keep God's commandments and sacrificed to foreign gods.

Their derogation became so great that God allowed their enemies—the ones they had wanted to mirror in worship—to destroy them and take them into captivity. Isn't this exactly what sin does to us today? It starts with a wrong motivation, attitude, or action and grows into a habit, lust, or obsession. Once the enemy has our full attention, he closes the trap, and we cannot shake free from the bondage. We are held captive as a result of our wayward actions.

We had to fight in the First World War, and we went through the Great Depression. Then there was the Second World War, then the Korean War, and we have fought in Vietnam and other conflicts since then. We battled the Communists for years. But I believe that we are now facing a threat that is much more serious than any enemy we have met in combat up to this point because it involves religion—and that makes it far more dangerous and disastrous. Don't be deceived into thinking that God would never allow anything to happen to the United States. He has a purpose that is far greater than ensuring our comfort and selfish desires.

We cannot defy His laws, ignore His principles, and act as if His commandments do not exist. To do so on any level—as a nation or as individuals—is to lay the foundation for spiritual suicide. We know so much; we have so much truth. The bottom line is that we are without excuse. God's people need to wake up and begin living the way He has called us to live—pure and holy lives that are totally committed to Him and His principles. God is not going to allow us to ignore Him without suffering the consequences of our sin. We may respond to this line of thinking very casually, but the truth is at some point—whether it is now or in our children's and grandchildren's generations—God will use whatever means necessary to get our attention. I don't like writing these words. I never enjoy telling them to my congregation, but to ignore them is to turn a deaf ear to the way God operates. He uses the wicked to punish sin.

Mission Fulfilled!

Before we close this chapter, I want to show how God did this very thing in the life of Jesus. First, He used Caesar Augustus to set the stage for the

Savior's place of birth. It was Augustus who made a decree stating that there would be a census taken and that everyone had to go back to the place where he was born. Joseph took Mary and headed to his hometown, which was Bethlehem. It was there that Jesus was born, which was the fulfillment of a very specific Old Testament prophecy (Micah 5:2). Second, Herod heard about His coming and passed a decree ordering that all children two years and under be killed. He was sure this act would take care of Christ's birth. But an angel of the Lord spoke to Joseph in a dream, warning him of the danger and telling him to take the baby and His mother into Egypt where they would be safe. So the family fled to Egypt and later, after the danger had passed, came back to Nazareth, where they lived.

When trouble comes or evil attacks, your smartest course of action is to ask God in prayer to show you what you need to do. If sin is involved, ask Him to forgive you. If this is not the case and you are just flat out under attack, then He will make this clear. Joseph and Mary were right in step with God's plan, but that did not prevent them from having to face a very wicked threat. It came because of the Messiah's birth. There was no way Satan was going to stand by and allow Jesus to grow up without a single threat. But notice what Joseph did: he obeyed God. More than likely he did not understand what was taking place. We never read that Joseph had perfect understanding about Christ's birth. But he knew enough to realize that he needed to do what God was instructing him to do. And the Lord preserved His Son—the Messiah.

At every turn in His life, Jesus faced some type of threat from the rulers of His day (Luke 20:19–20). The Pharisees and the Sadducees trumped up charges against Him. Pilate condemned Him to death. And the Romans were the ones who physically crucified Him. If we consider the life of Jesus, we find that the religious leaders of His day were determined to kill Him. They were motivated by hatred and selfish ambition that centered on their religious views. They missed the coming of the Messiah because Jesus did not fit their description of what the Savior should be. He was not a political man, which was what they were seeking in the Messiah—a man who would free them from Roman rule and oppression. The eyes of their hearts were set not on God but on themselves. To them, freedom was not a spiritual issue. It was a political problem, but Jesus came for a different reason. He did not come so that He could be an earthly king. He came to save us from an eternal death. God used the wicked to put His Son on a cross and then in a grave, but death had no power over Him. The grave is empty, and we can have eternal life through faith in Jesus Christ.

The Lord used every wicked, evil plot to accomplish His purpose, which was to bring the Redeemer into this world. Later the same pattern was at work in the lives of the disciples. The more Peter and the apostles preached the gospel message, the more they were persecuted (Acts 5). And with every event, God was narrowing their focus, drawing them closer to Himself, and strengthening them to do the work He created them to do. Many died because of their faith, but they did not leave this earth without fulfilling the mission that they had been given to do.

Although the enemy attacks and seeks to destroy God's people, he will never reach his goal. He is a defeated foe. He was sure that he had a foothold in the life of Saul, but after the death of Stephen, God saved this man on the Damascus Road. He also gave him a new name, a new passion, and a new occupation—Saul became Paul—an apostle of the Lord Jesus Christ. His life was changed, but until he met the Savior, evil stalked him, filling his mind with lies and thoughts that were not in keeping with God's will or plan.

In Acts, Luke reported that Saul stood by and watched the stoning of Stephen—in essence he gave his approval to what was done (Acts 7). Why did God allow this to take place? Only the Lord knows, but I can tell you what I believe was one of the positive results for the New Testament church that came from the persecution of Saul and others like him. It is this: the testimony and witness of God's truth began to be told throughout the known world. The early church was strengthened—not weakened—by persecution.

Jesus had instructed His followers to take His gospel message to the world. However, after His resurrection, they lingered in Jerusalem and had a wonderful time of fellowship and talking about all that they had witnessed during His lifetime. God had to use extreme measures to motivate them to leave the city and obey His command. So, He allowed persecution. Like Stephen, many were stoned. Others were forced to leave family and friends and move to other regions. Nero was the emperor, and he was extremely committed to killing and expelling as many Jews from Rome as possible. This is how the gospel message began to spread.

Believers fled for safety or were banished from cities, and wherever they went, they told others about the saving grace of the Lord Jesus Christ. Over his lifetime, Paul faced numerous difficulties. God did not spare him from them. Many times, he ended up in prison. You may think, *I have never understood why God allowed him to spend so much time in jail.* The answer is easy to surmise. Paul's schedule was full. The Lord allowed him to spend time in prison so he could write. That was where he wrote Ephesians, Colossians, Philippians, Philemon, Romans, and 1 and 2 Corinthians. We call these books of the Bible the Prison Epistles, and each one contains valuable lessons about who God is and how we are to live.

We think something is unfair or cruel, but the Lord knows its potential value. We may feel as though it is unfair or a mistake, but God sees it fitting perfectly into His plan. If Paul had been a free man, he probably would have been so caught up in preaching the gospel and starting churches that he never would have written the letters to the various churches that he established. These church letters, or books, make up a huge portion of the New Testament. This is solely my conjecture, but I believe God put him in prison so that he could record His principles that would be given to His people. Wicked, self-motivated leaders believed they had taken him off the scene, yet that was far from being true. He was in the hub of action and positioned perfectly to instruct not only those of his day but also millions of people generations later, for we are still reading and studying the words God gave him to write.

We know the Lord uses righteous deeds and people to accomplish His will. But it can be very difficult for some people to understand how He uses the wicked to accomplish His purposes. It is much more inviting to consider how He uses good things to shape our lives rather than evil or sorrow to mold and to prepare us for His service. However, I can say without hesitation that my greatest lessons of faith have come through times of extreme difficulty—times when I felt persecuted, betrayed, or rejected. I also can say that each and every single time when I looked back at those events, I could see the hand of God at work, guiding me and preparing me for a tremendous blessing.

The same is true for you. It may seem as though your world has caved in around you, but nothing is outside God's omnipotent ability. He can redeem, recover, and restore all that has been lost in a far greater way than you can ever imagine. It may not look exactly the same, but I can assure you that when He is involved, it will be even better than anything you have experienced.

Peter wrote with a knowing pen,

> Be of sober spirit, be on the alert. Your adversary, the devil, prowls around like a roaring lion, seeking someone to devour. But resist him, firm in your faith, knowing that the same experiences of suffering are being accomplished by your brethren who are in the world. After you have suffered for a little while, the God of all grace, who called you to His eternal glory in Christ, will Himself perfect, confirm, strengthen and establish you. (1 Peter 5:8–10)

God never allows us to face adversity longer than it takes to accomplish His purpose. Israel entered the promised land, and you will, too, if you will set the eyes of your heart like a flint on pleasing the One who gave Himself for you (Isa. 50:7).

Chapter Six

EXPECT THE UNEXPECTED

I love surprises, but I also enjoy surprising those I know and love. This is just one of the reasons I enjoy Christmas. While it provides the right occasion for us to stop and consider the greatest gift that has ever been given to mankind, the gift of God's Son, it also is a time when we can watch those we love open gifts that have been carefully selected for them. We express our joy, love, and gratitude to those who mean so much to us. When my children were young, I would stay up late on Christmas Eve putting together doll houses, train sets, or some miniature log construction toy that was sure to be embraced or turned on through shrills of joyous laughter. Snapping together the pieces of the toys, I would mentally imagine Andy's and Becky's faces the following morning. The thought of wonder and surprise in their eyes always motivated me to give to them. And it still does.

Do you like surprises—things that show up suddenly and fill you with a sense of awe and wonder? God knows exactly what we long to have. He knows the needs and desires of our hearts, and He wants us to trust Him fully to give good things to us because we are His children (Matt. 7:11). Often His gifts come in the form of a surprise visit. Do you enjoy opening the door and being surprised by someone who has dropped by for a visit? You may laugh and think, *Well, it depends on who it is.* I understand this line of thinking. Some people don't like surprise visits for the simple reason that it makes them nervous. They want to make sure the house is clean before their visitor shows up at the door. We cannot prepare for surprises. Sometimes, people just drop by to see us. Depending on who it is—close friends or family—we may feel perfectly fine. But what do you do when a stranger or someone you respect greatly shows up? You could feel very uncomfortable, or you could be filled with joy.

There are times when God shows up in our lives without any prior announcement. Suddenly we become aware of His presence. A skeptic may say, "I don't believe that He shows up anymore. Saying you can sense His closeness is not a reality. Only weak-minded people think this way." My heart breaks when I hear these words because I know that person is missing something absolutely awesome—a personal relationship with the Lord Jesus Christ. Throughout this book, we are studying God's ways—His motives, His plans, and His goals for our lives. We have discussed that He always has a specific purpose for all that He does, and that includes His surprise visits. At these times we know that He is speaking particularly to us. Through various ways, He lets us know that He is extremely aware of our devotion, love, commitment, and circumstances.

After His resurrection, Jesus surprised His followers on several occasions by stepping into the very center of their confusion and heartache. There have been times in my life when I have been battling an issue, and even though I have prayed and committed the situation or problem to the Lord, a little nagging reminder of its intensity has remained. Then I have gone back to the Lord in prayer and admitted my frustration: "Lord, I don't know how to handle this. One way seems right, but I realize You know what is best." Prayer always corrects the focus of my heart and mind. If my thinking is not in line with God's, He usually lets me know because He understands that my greatest desire is to please Him. On more than one occasion, He has answered me by speaking directly to my spirit with two very simple but assuring words, *Trust Me*. The moment I sense Him saying this, I relax because I know that this is one way He reminds me that He has everything in control and that He is concerned about me. The same is true for you. The psalmist wrote these encouraging words:

> Trust in the LORD and do good;
> Dwell in the land and cultivate faithfulness.
> Delight yourself in the LORD;
> And He will give you the desires of your heart.
> Commit your way to the LORD,
> Trust also in Him, and He will do it.
> He will bring forth your righteousness as the light
> And your judgment as the noonday. (Ps. 37:3–6)

God has never failed to keep a single promise. If He tells you to trust Him, you can absolutely put your faith in Him and know whatever concerns you concerns Him and He will work on your behalf. You do not need to worry, fret, or wonder what you should do next because when it is time for you to take a step, He will make it perfectly clear. And one of the ways He does this is by showing up in your life.

God Steps into Our Circumstances

Following the Crucifixion, Mary Magdalene approached Christ's tomb, but she realized something was wrong. The massive stone that had been rolled into place covering the opening to the sepulcher had been moved. Scholars wonder how the women planned to move it so that they could reach the body of the Lord. But God provided the answer. Immediately she ran back to the place where the other disciples were and told Peter and John what she had seen. When they returned to the garden tomb and found that it was empty, Mary was overcome with grief. The others left the area, but she remained behind, weeping:

> As she wept, she stooped and looked into the tomb; and she saw two angels in white sitting, one at the head and one at the feet, where the body of Jesus had been lying. And they said to her, "Woman, why are you weeping?" She said to them, "Because they have taken away my Lord, and I do not know where they have laid Him." When she had said this, she turned around and saw Jesus standing there, and did not know that it was Jesus.
>
> Jesus said to her, "Woman, why are you weeping? Whom are you seeking?" Supposing Him to be the gardener, she said to Him, "Sir, if you have carried Him away, tell me where you have laid Him, and I will take Him away." Jesus said to her, "Mary!" She turned and said to Him in Hebrew, "Rabboni!" (which means, Teacher). (John 20:11–16)

In verse 9, we read, "They did not understand the Scripture, that He must rise again from the dead." Even though Jesus had taught about the need for His death and resurrection, no one grasped the concept of the need for His crucifixion. They did not understand why He had to die, and they viewed the entire event from a human perspective. His appearance to Mary was a surprise visit. He showed up with important news and words of encouragement. The hope they had experienced during His earthly lifetime had been more than dashed. It had been eliminated. That is, until the resurrection, when Jesus began to appear to those who loved Him. In this case, it was Mary who saw Him first. His compassion for her at the sight of her grief could not be contained, and He surprised her by revealing His true nature to her.

God's love for you and me is not a mystery. His desire is not to hide or make His will and plan difficult to discern. Mary's focus was on God's

Son—*Where is He? How can I find Him? Tell me so I can take care of His body.* God's heart is moved with compassion when He sees devotion of this level. You may not see two angels before you, but I can assure you that if you truly long to know His mind about a particular situation, He will answer you. He won't leave you standing on the sidelines of life questioning whether or not you have done the right thing.

Often our greatest consideration is how something will affect us. We want to see life unfold according to what we deem as being right. Imagine what life would be like if God's ways were based on our desires and feelings. There would be nothing but chaos in our world. Have you ever been in a position where you have wondered, *God, where are You? Can't You see that I'm sinking— going under and don't think that I will be able to rebound from this dark emotional state?* Suddenly God sends someone to you with words of encouragement. He is breaking through the darkness you feel, telling you not to give up. The messenger may be human, but the communication is from God. Or He may simply speak to your spirit—just a single word or two that strike a nerve deep within you and light a small fire of hope. *Trust Me* are just two of the words that He often uses to encourage me when I need to know that all is well. He also speaks to us through His Word. We may be reading something that seems totally unrelated to the circumstances of our lives. Suddenly the words seem written expressly for our problem or situation. This happens a lot when we are praying for guidance and need God's wisdom so that we can make the right decision. Just when we need to know that what we are doing is right, God speaks to our hearts.

We need to remember several things concerning these encounters with God.

God's Surprise Visits Always Have a Purpose

It is essential to remember this, especially when our world becomes upended. If we fail to keep an eternal perspective, we could run the risk of being deeply disappointed or discouraged. God promised Abraham that he would have a son (Gen. 17). But he had to wait years before he saw the promise become a reality. We can only imagine the joy that he and Sarah experienced over Isaac's birth. A few years later, the Lord called to him, but the message was not one of joy and delight: "Take now your son, your only son, whom you love, Isaac, and go to the land of Moriah, and offer him there as a burnt offering on one of the mountains of which I will tell you" (Gen. 22:2). Just when Isaac had grown to an age where he could travel with his father, listen to his stories of faith in God, and understand a hint of his miraculous birth, God gave Abraham a directive that none of us would expect or want to hear. He told him to take his son and travel to a place where he would offer the boy as a sacrifice.

That was the only information he was given—no reasons explaining why or any future promise. The only instruction sheet contained deeply disturbing words. Yet in the next verse, we read, "So Abraham rose early in the morning and saddled his donkey, and took two of his young men with him and Isaac his son; and he split wood for the burnt offering, and arose and went to the place of which God had told him" (v. 3). Notice what Abraham did not try to do. He did not seek to talk God out of His decision. Though it had to be the hardest thing he had done, he went out and split enough wood for the sacrifice and began the journey. His obedience was sorely tested, and he passed the test.

God called Abraham His *friend* (Isa. 41:8), confirming what Abraham knew—that God's love and providential care were infinite. Just as he was about to sacrifice Isaac, the Lord called to him, "Abraham, Abraham! . . . Do not stretch out your hand against the lad, and do nothing to him; for now I know that you fear God, since you have not withheld your son, your only son, from Me" (Gen. 22:11–12). The only thing that mattered to Abraham was doing what God instructed him to do. There will be times when He will motivate us to do something we do not understand.

If we trust Him, not only will we see how He works everything out for our good, but also we will remain right in step with His plan for our lives.

God Wants to Make His Will Clear to Us

Sometimes, life is a step-by-step process. The Lord tells you to step forward by faith and you do, but you also may wonder, *What's next?* Many times, He gives us only enough light and understanding to take one step at a time. He knows that if He reveals His entire plan to us, we might become afraid, discouraged, or in some cases, prideful. I often caution those who come to me seeking advice never to assume they know what God wants them to do. It is important to be in step with His plan, even if it moves faster or slower than the pace they would choose.

Although we cannot know all there is to know about God's will, He will reveal enough so that we will know exactly what to do. One woman expressed total frustration over her circumstances: "I just don't understand. How can God allow this to happen? Doesn't He know that I have trained for a management position? But here I am—stuck in what appears to be a dead-end job." Many times, God's goal for our lives is simply to be willing to be still and content with what He has given. In times of stillness, we learn to trust Him and also have the opportunity to grow deeper in our relationship with Him.

You can't run at a fast pace for long and maintain a close, intimate relationship with the Savior. Jesus made sure that He took time to be with the heavenly Father. His earthly ministry was extremely important. In fact, that was why He came to earth, to do the Father's will. But He could not fulfill God's plan if He was always on the move, always rushing, and never being still in God's presence. The Lord will show you exactly what you need to do and when you need to do it. But before this can take place, you must learn to be still and look for His coming.

God Expects Obedience

God's surprise visits often come in response to our obedience. He may show up when we have strayed from His will, but He also surprises us when we are walking right in step with His plan. There is a tremendous sense of joy waiting for all who desire nothing more than to worship and live for Him. You don't have to be in the ministry to do this. And you really don't have to be in a special location to worship God, though I do believe that each one of us needs to learn how to pray and be quiet before Him. In fact, even though our schedules can be overwhelming at times, the wisest thing we can do is to pray each morning before we start our days. I have talked with moms and dads who say there is no way they can do this. They are up late at night with small children, and then they are on the run all day. But I believe that if we ask Him, God will help us carve out the minutes when we can stop and pray. This is the most important thing we will do. We cannot adequately meet the demands of our world, jobs, and relationships without God's wisdom. The Son of God could not do this, and neither can we.

"I'm too tired to pray," one single mother told me. She went on to explain that there were times when she felt as though every area of her life was out of control. I suggested that she start small. In other words, keep her expectations realistic. Since she had a job and young children to get ready for school, forty-five minutes in prayer could seem too much. So, she began with twenty minutes of quiet time in the morning. She also found that she could easily pray about the day's activities and for others who were hurting or had a need. Soon I noticed that her countenance had lifted. She also reported that she was reading her Bible before turning off her light at night. Her obedience was marked by an increase in her ability to get everything done on her schedule. God economizes our time when we set our hearts on knowing Him and obeying His commandments. Try putting Him first for thirty days and see if you do not have more time in your schedule and also the wisdom to make solid decisions at home, on your job, and anywhere else.

God's Surprise Visits Are Always Blessings

If we could ask Abraham, Isaiah, David, Paul, Peter, John, Moses, Mary, and Martha how they felt about the miraculous work of their Lord, I can imagine every one of these people and countless others would say the same thing. Nothing compares to suddenly being wrapped up in the awareness of God's presence. Even when He has a word of correction, it is awesome to know that He desires to speak to you and me. Not only this, but He loves us and wants to use us for His glory.

Standing before the burning bush, Moses removed his sandals and fell on his face in worship. After hearing God's plan, did he shrug his shoulders and go back to doing what he had done for years? No. His life was eternally changed from being in God's presence. He went back to Midian, packed up his bedroll, grabbed Aaron, and headed to Pharaoh's palace. God had surprised him and changed his life and destiny. One reason God spoke to Moses in such an awesome way is that He was calling him to do something that would test Moses in every area.

The enemy has very little interest in a nonbeliever. If the enemy has succeeded in sufficiently blinding someone to the truth, love, and mercy of God, he is not going to be concerned about how degenerate the person's life becomes. He spins a wicked web of lust, anger, bitterness, depression, and much more. Once a person falls into it, she is caught—trapped—and Satan is satisfied. But when eyes are opened and a person comes to know Jesus Christ as Savior and Lord, the playing field changes. Suddenly there is a real, viable threat working against the kingdom of darkness. The enemy knows he is a defeated foe, but he certainly does not want anyone else understanding this.

God's surprise visit to Moses set in motion a chain of events that are still unfolding today. Everything God does has a purpose and eternal value. If we scan biblical history, we see God at work, stepping onto the scene exactly when He is needed, giving guidance, wisdom, and encouragement. He moves through the lives of men and women who are available to be used by Him. Then He sends His blessings. Goals are reached, lives are changed, relationships are mended, and intimacy grows between Him and us.

Getting Ready for Change

A very important reason that God visits us is to prepare us for some future event. On several occasions, I have mentioned how He spoke to my heart before He moved me to Atlanta. I had been the senior pastor in a church in Bartow, Florida, for eleven months. Even though I loved the church and the area, and I had no desire to move, I sensed a growing restlessness in my spirit. I tried to dismiss it, yet it kept resurfacing. Then when I was out of town preaching a revival, God got my attention.

The constant feeling that change was on the way motivated me to pray for an answer to why I was feeling the way I did. One evening after the service, I decided to go back to my room and spend time alone with Him in prayer. I had to know what He wanted to say to me. I pulled out a legal pad and listed several areas where I thought God could be working. At the end of my list, I placed a question mark on a line by itself. In other words, there was something that He was doing, but I did not know what it was.

After the service on the following night, I returned to my room and began to pray, but before I could utter very many words, I sensed God's Spirit say, *I'm going to move you.* That was it. I asked, "When?" and in my mind's eye, I saw the word *September.* I returned to my home in Bartow after the revival. The next Monday morning, a friend who lived in Atlanta called me. He was a member of a search committee at First Baptist. He opened our conversation by saying, "I want to talk to you about something that you have never con-sidered." The moment I heard those words, I thought back to what God had told me a few days earlier. He asked me to consider becoming the associate pastor at First Baptist Atlanta. We talked a little longer, and I explained that I would not be interested because I loved where I was and I didn't want to step back to being an associate pastor. The moment I hung up the telephone, I burst into tears and thought, *Lord, what are You doing?*

A couple of weeks later, members from the pulpit committee at First Baptist Atlanta came for a visit. They repeated the job offer, and I reassured them that I was not interested in moving my family to Atlanta. However, they continued to call me and say that every time they prayed, my name was the only one that kept coming up! Finally they visited me again, and this time the senior pastor accompanied them. He asked, "What is God going to have to do [to get you to say yes]?" I answered, "He is going to have to make it crystal clear." That was exactly what He did in the days that followed as I continued to pray and read His Word. I knew when I packed the car to move that I was in the center of His will, and that was all that mattered. My happiness at that point came as a result of my desire to sur-render to His plan and forsake my comfort and pleasure. By September, I moved to Atlanta, Georgia, and within a few weeks I was in my office at the First Baptist Church.

There is another point to this story: God knows how to gain our attention. He knows the right combination of words or events to motivate us to stop and ask, "Lord, what are You saying to me? Show me Your will so I may do it." I think about Abraham, and most of the times God called to him, he answered, "Here I am" (Gen. 22:11). There wasn't any fussing or fuming or questioning God. "God tested Abraham, and said to him, 'Abraham!' And he said, 'Here I am'" (Gen. 22:1).

What is your first reaction to God's call? Is it, "Lord, I am here. I want to hear Your voice"? Do you want to run because you are not convinced that doing His will is the best thing? Remember Jonah; he ran, but he could not outrun God.

I never would have believed that I would be in Atlanta within such a short period of time, but that was exactly what happened. Time is not a factor to God. He can use a short amount of time to accomplish a great deal, or He may choose to have us wait a long time before revealing His will or plan. His goals are always to motivate us to move closer to Him and to learn how to trust Him in greater ways. We will never reach a point where we know all there is to know about God. It is impossible because He is omniscient—He knows everything, and there is no beginning or end to His righteousness, holiness, and love for you and me. God also allows us to experience a portion of His presence through His Holy Spirit and in times when He speaks to our hearts. When God shows up, we should bow down.

Think about the tremendous responsibility given to Joshua. Moses was dead, and he had the task of leading the people into the promised land. The Lord surely knew that he felt the burden of the awesome task that he had been given to do. Before the nation of Israel was scheduled to march on the city of Jericho, Joshua was alone near the city:

> He lifted up his eyes and looked, and behold, a man was standing opposite him with his sword drawn in his hand, and Joshua went to him and said, "Are you for us or for our adversaries?"
>
> He said, "No; rather I indeed come now as captain of the host of the Lord." And Joshua fell on his face to the earth, and bowed down, and said to him, "What has my lord to say to his servant?" The captain of the Lord's host said to Joshua, "Remove your sandals from your feet, for the place where you are standing is holy." And Joshua did so. (Josh. 5:13–15)

I don't imagine it took any time for him to remove his shoes, for the simple reason that Moses probably told him how God had called to him from the burning bush. That surprise visit led to Moses becoming the redeemer of the nation of Israel. Joshua was experiencing the same thing—only this time, God's platform was not a burning bush; it was the commander of His heavenly armies. Joshua, like Moses, was standing in the awesome presence of holy God.

We are never outside His presence. His Spirit lives within us, but the whole world and all that the universe contains are His. He made Joshua aware of His closeness, and then He began to give him the strategy for battle. God was preparing him for the next step. And often the way He will do this for us is by stepping into our world of problems, issues, trials, and challenges. He is just as likely to show up when everything seems to be going well and there is nothing that needs our attention. Many times, I have sensed His closeness and joy in my life. Other times, when conflict increased and my ability to cope was stretched, He abruptly spoke to my heart so that I would be encouraged or guided in a certain direction.

We may not always understand God's reasoning. He was about to tell Joshua something that did not fit his military training or genius. All the years that he had served alongside Moses, he had never marched around a city wall without speaking a word. The fact is, he probably never would have thought of walking around the city of Jericho without devising a frontal attack. But God laid out a completely different plan from the one he was accustomed to doing. It was not to advance, fight, and conquer. It was to advance by faith in God and then to walk with a sincere trust in His ability over the enemy. The victory was going to be a result of people marching, blowing trumpets, and shouting to God's glory, which from the perspective of a military leader made no sense at all.

When God points you in a direction that goes against human reasoning, it is always a good idea to stop and ask Him to make His will clear to you. He may or may not choose to do this. Then you need to make a decision about whether you are listening to your imagination or the Lord.

Joshua did not argue with God. He did not respond to Him by saying, "Moses and I did not operate that way. Here is what we did." No. Instead, he got up after his encounter and prepared to go into battle the way that God had instructed. At times, His plans and methods will not make sense. That is why we say that we live by faith and not by sight (2 Cor. 5:7). There was no other way for Joshua to live. The same was true for the nation of Israel. Once they received their walking instructions, they had only one option for blessing, and that was obedience. Anything else would have resulted in disappointment and fear.

I believe one reason why so many Christians are battling fear and anxiety is that they do not have enough faith to trust God in times of distress, challenge, or difficulty. This was a defining moment for Joshua and the nation of Israel because they had to lay aside their strategy and follow a very unfamiliar course of action. Usually God will allow us to witness Him at work before He asks us to do something that seems so far away from what we believe to be practical. He builds our faith, but He also brings us to a point where we *must* trust Him. There is absolutely no other way.

Time and time again, Joshua witnessed God at work. He had been a part of the group that had crossed the Red Sea. He had been close by when Moses struck the rock and water flowed from it. He had watched the Lord provide for the needs of a massive number of people. Now he was standing at the threshold to the promised land again, and there was only one thing for him to do—trust God. He was one of the twelve original spies, one of two men who returned with a favorable report and urged the people to "by all means go up and take possession of it, for we will surely overcome it" (Num. 13:30). But the people rebelled against the Lord then. As a result of their sin, the nation spent forty years in the wilderness wandering from one campsite to another.

When you look at a map and chart the course of Israel, you find that it amounts to nothing more than a very large circle. An entire generation passed away, except for Joshua and Caleb, before God allowed the people to enter the land He had reserved as a promised blessing. This is what we want to avoid doing—traveling in circles and suffering heartache. Yet I meet people who have chosen to resist God's will even after He shows up in their lives in a mighty way. They continue to say no to His plan, and their lives are outlined with misery, disappointment, and failure. He loves them, but His blessings are limited because He cannot and will not bless sin or disobedience. Yet He is moved to action when He sees our faith in Him growing.

God's Words Are Instructional

In Joshua 6 we read, "Now Jericho was tightly shut because of the sons of Israel; no one went out and no one came in. The Lord said to Joshua, 'See, I have given Jericho into your hand, with its king and the valiant warriors'" (vv. 1–2). Before Joshua and the people even approached Jericho's walls, God made it clear that He had given them the city. His surprise visits often are points of encouragement—letting us know that He is the One who has brought us to this point and the One who will lead us to victory. We need to know that when we have made the right choice, taken the right step, said no to sin, or chosen to follow a path that our friends would not have taken, God is pleased and honored by our actions. His encouragement keeps us moving forward when we are tempted to look at the rising waves or shrink back in fear when winds of adversity begin to blow.

The enemy will tempt us to think about what we have done. Satan watches to see how we respond to a challenge or an idea. If we set our sights on reaching the goal, he will do his level best to discourage us and tempt us into giving up. Surely Joshua had to deal with the enormity of the task he had been given to do, but it was not as hard as he first envisioned, knowing that

God already had settled the entire matter. Jericho was conquered. The walls fell, and Israel had obeyed the Lord.

This is one of the reasons why we should never set limits on God's ability. After all, is anything too difficult for Him (Jer. 32:27)? He can take what we feel is insignificant and of very little value and work through it in a mighty way. Gideon's encounter with the Lord is another example of how He surprises us and changes the atmosphere of our hopelessness into one of vital potential and victory. God appeared to Gideon as an angel: "The angel of the LORD appeared to him and said to him, 'The LORD is with you, O valiant warrior'" (Judg. 6:12). Immediately the Lord addressed him from a positive perspective. He understood that Gideon and the nation of Israel were in dire circumstances. He also knew that the hearts of the people were filled with dread. Their enemies were oppressing them. Therefore, Gideon answered God with words that reflected a heavy heart: "O my lord, if the LORD is with us, why then has all this happened to us? And where are all His miracles which our fathers told us about, saying, 'Did not the LORD bring us up from Egypt?' But now the LORD has abandoned us and given us into the hand of Midian" (v. 13). From Gideon's position, the future looked very bleak and was getting more dismal with each day.

The Midianites had a habit of coming into the land where Israel lived, and they would destroy the crops "and leave no sustenance in Israel as well as no sheep, ox, or donkey. For they would come up with their livestock and their tents, they would come in like locusts for number, both they and their camels were innumerable; and they came into the land to devastate it. So Israel was brought very low because of Midian, and the sons of Israel cried to the LORD" (vv. 6:4–6).

But there is another side to the story. God had instructed Israel to worship only Him. Period. Yet the people had adopted the religious views of their enemies and the pagan nations around them. While they continued to worship God, they added the worship of Baal and constructed a representation of Ashtaroth, a female deity, a consort of Baal, and the goddess of war and fertility. Many pagan cultures worshiped her. In Greece, her title was Aphrodite, and in Rome, she was the goddess Venus. These were fertility goddesses, and worship to such false deities often involved prostitution and child sacrifice.

Therefore, Israel was definitely not living a pure existence before the Lord. However, God heard the cries of the people. We must never forget that He will always keep His promises. We experience the painful consequences of our sin, but in time, God will do exactly what He has said He would do. His promise to Israel was to take them into the land that He had provided for them. Nothing about His initial promise to Abraham had changed. The only thing that continued to prevent it from taking place was the people's determination to worship and live any way they pleased. And we can certainly see how this sinful attitude is still in operation today. Without a doubt, we suffer whenever we assume we know more than God and step away from the path that He has chosen for us to follow.

God did not lecture Gideon concerning his remarks about His ability. He knew Gideon's heart and said, "Go in this your strength and deliver Israel from the hand of Midian. Have I not sent you?" (Judg. 6:14). We often know what the Lord wants us to do, but we hesitate. We recall past disappointments and wonder if the same will be repeated. We fail to see that

- God has a specific time for everything to take place.

- Regardless of our circumstances, He is in control.

- We stop trusting Him when trouble or painful situations continue over a long period of time.

- We look at what others have and think, *Why not me, Lord?*

When God makes His presence known, especially when we have battled difficulty for a long time, we may be tempted to respond the way Gideon did by asking Him to repeatedly confirm His will to us. The best way to handle feelings that turn cynical is to stop and ask God to show us if we are thinking correctly or if we have drifted in our faith by believing Satan's lies. Far too often, people end up trapped in circumstances that consume them and prevent them from doing what God instructed them to do because they refuse to lift their eyes and see the potential that is theirs through Jesus Christ. God's calling to Israel had not changed. However, the people had allowed their hearts to become darkened by sin, disobedience, and the worship of foreign gods.

Gideon's story is familiar to many people. He laid a fleece out before the Lord, and he said, "If there is dew on the fleece only, and it is dry on all the ground, then I will know that You will deliver Israel through me, as You have spoken" (Judg. 6:37). That was exactly what God did—wet fleece and dry ground. But Gideon still did not believe that what he had heard was from the Lord. And the fact was, the angel of the Lord—God Himself—had spoken to Gideon. But instead of trusting Him fully, Gideon went back a second time and said, "Please let me make a test once more with the fleece, let it now be dry only on the fleece, and let there be dew on all the ground" (v. 39). In all fairness, Gideon had faced several exhausting defeats. God's surprise visit was difficult for him to understand because the Lord was asking him to do something that he felt was impossible—to fight Midian and win. There will be times when God does the same thing for us. We may be looking for Him to work in a certain way, and we refuse to step out in faith.

Years ago, when we were trusting God at In Touch to provide the funds for the construction of a new building, I became convinced that we should not borrow any money. The temptation to move ahead and call the bank was great because the desire to broadcast God's gospel message to the world was heartfelt and strong. But we chose to wait because we felt that God wanted us to do that. Each member of my executive team agreed that God would provide the money for us to continue to grow. Once that issue was settled, we began to wait for Him to provide for us. When His timing was right, we had the money we needed to build and expand. Over the years, this has been an overriding theme for our work: obey God and leave all the consequences to Him.

The Lord understands our doubts and fear. He understands why we fail to believe Him, why we hesitate to obey, and why we look at a situation as Gideon did, recalling past defeats instead of looking ahead to potential victories. But none of this changes God's mind or directives. He led Gideon into battle but not the way he envisioned. Instead of allowing him to have a huge army at his disposal, his forces were reduced to a mere three hundred fighting men. Gideon allowed twenty-two thousand to return home because they were afraid of the Midianites, and then God separated and divided the number that remained until all that was left of Israel's army was a small band of committed soldiers. But they were enough. Gideon had seen the angel of the Lord, and this completely changed his perspective: "When Gideon saw that he was the angel of the LORD, he said, 'Alas, O Lord GOD! For now I have seen the angel of the LORD face to face'" (Judg. 6:22).

As the men were preparing for battle, God allowed Gideon to slip into the Midianite camp, where he discovered that the enemy soldiers were paralyzed with fear. They had heard that the power of God was with Israel and especially with Gideon. They also believed that Israel's army was far greater than theirs. By the next morning, Israel did not even have to walk on to the battlefield. The night before, God led them to devise a plot that confused the enemy in their own camp. Israel blew trumpets, smashed pitchers, and created so much noise that their enemies were sure that they were surrounded by a great army. They were so frightened by this surprise attack that they escaped in fear (Judg. 7:9–25). God gained the victory and the people learned an important lesson concerning His ways and His faithfulness.

Do you look for God's surprise visits, or do you dodge Him and ignore His call to you? Probably one of the most well-known surprise visits involved Mary and the angel of the Lord who foretold the Savior's birth: "Now in the sixth month the angel Gabriel was sent from God to a city in Galilee called Nazareth, to a virgin engaged to a man whose name was Joseph, of the descendants of David; and the virgin's name was Mary. And coming in, he said to her, 'Greetings, favored one! The Lord is with you'" (Luke 1:26–28). The angel announced who he was and then told Mary what would happen over the course of the next few months and thirty-three years. I don't believe she ever forgot what it felt like to stand in the presence of God's messenger and to hear His words spoken to her.

We are not going to experience His surprise visits on a regular basis. We can sense the presence of His Spirit in our lives, but visits like the ones listed here do not happen frequently. When they do, we remember exactly what God says to us. Mary could not imagine how she would have a son since she was a virgin: "How can this be . . . ?" (v. 34). But the angel was quick to point out that "nothing will be impossible with God" (v. 37).

You may be standing at what appears to be a dead end. Or you may have just received such disappointing news that you are wondering how you will continue. There is only one way, and that is by remembering that God's love for you is infinite, unconditional, and long-suffering. When you face sorrow and adversity, He faces it with you. When you are forced to walk through a valley that seems to be without end, He willingly goes out before you holding the light of His love so that you will not stumble in darkness.

His surprise visits are like exclamation marks placed along our way, reminding us that He has a plan and He will not abandon us because He has created us in love and for a purpose. We can drift in our devotion to Him as Israel did, but we cannot stop or prevent Him from accomplishing His will. Mary's future belonged to the Lord. She said,

> My soul exalts the Lord,
> And my spirit has rejoiced in God my Savior.
> For He has had regard for the humble state of His bondslave. . . .
> He has given help to Israel His servant,
> In remembrance of His mercy,
> As He spoke to our fathers,
> To Abraham and his descendants forever. (Luke 1:46–48, 54–55)

Mary's focus was set—fixed on the Lord—and it never changed.

Zacharias, who was a priest and would become the father of John the Baptist, also received a visit from an angel (Luke 1:13–16). That was an awesome surprise. His son would become the forerunner of the Messiah and the man who would announce the coming of the Lord. His encounter was so punctuated by the fact that God had spoken to him, the Lord chose to silence Zacharias's voice until the birth of his son. Once the baby boy was born, Zacharias asked for a tablet and wrote, "His name is John." That was the name given to him by God on the day of the angel's visit. Immediately "his mouth was opened and his tongue loosed, and he began to speak in praise of God" (v. 64).

Why was a surprise visit necessary? In each one of these situations, the outcome that God had planned was difficult for the people to believe. Mary was a virgin, Gideon was outnumbered, Zacharias knew his wife was barren, and Joshua was overwhelmed by the task placed before him. But these were the very situations that God chose to draw close to those who would accomplish His work. Whenever He speaks to you, the best thing you can do is listen and obey.

- Don't try to figure God out.

- Don't seek to limit God. Remember, His ways are higher than ours.

- Don't assume what God will do and not do.

On the Road to Emmaus

Once Passover and the Crucifixion were over, the people began to return to their homes. Cleopas and a friend left Jerusalem with heavy hearts and confused minds. They had just witnessed the death of Jesus Christ. The Bible tells us that they were disciples—followers of the Savior. As they walked, they talked about all they had witnessed over the past few days. I'm sure it was a heart-wrenching account. But it seems that the most important fact was omitted from their conversation, and that was how the prophets had foretold that this very thing would take place (Luke 24:25). Instead of asking, "God, what are You doing?" or "What do You want us to learn in these very difficult times?" they were focused on their loss and the hardship of being in such an unstable political climate.

While they walked, a stranger who was actually the Lord joined them, but they did not recognize Him. The fact is, they were shocked to learn He was so unaware of the events that had taken place over the past few days (Luke 24:18). We can become so consumed with our problems and situations that we can miss or overlook the Savior's approach. Jesus remained with the men. He could see the sadness on their faces, and He realized the shock was more than they could handle on their own. After He listened to them recount their experience and the anguish they had felt, He opened their minds to God's truth.

Jesus traced God's faithfulness to Israel and mankind. He started with His call to Moses and took them through the Old Testament. When they reached Emmaus, the two men urged Him to stay and have dinner with them. He agreed and once they settled around the table, Jesus picked up the bread and broke it, and "their eyes were opened and they recognized Him; and He vanished from their sight" (vv. 30–31). God came to them in the midst of their heartache—mental and emotional pain so strong, it had blinded them to the very fact that God was with them. The two disciples returned to Jerusalem and to the eleven with the news of Christ's resurrection. Word of other appearances soon reached Peter and the others.

It was not a one-time event. Jesus had risen. Peter had seen the empty grave, and he recalled the Savior's words before His death, but he did not have the ability to understand what had actually happened. Then Jesus stepped into their presence—probably the Upper Room or a place where they felt safe. Even though the doors were bolted and the curtains shut, Christ appeared to them. "They were startled and frightened and thought that they were seeing a spirit," but it was the Lord (v. 37). After they recognized Him, there was instant joy (v. 41) because He was with them again.

God knows when we need reassurance and direction. He knows when sorrow reaches a point of being overwhelming and debilitating. But even in times of adversity, we must choose to believe and open our eyes to His coming and to the truth He offers us. If we become mired in feelings of anger, distrust, and fear, we miss the opportunity to see Him and hear His words of comfort, correction, and promise for the future.

God shows up at key times. Saul encountered Him on the road to Damascus and came away a changed man. Much of the New Testament was written by this man—someone whom God saved and then renamed for His glory. The apostle Paul did more to spread the gospel of Jesus Christ than anyone else. He suffered greatly for the sake of the gospel, but I'm sure that the one thing he never forgot was the impact of his meeting with the Savior (Acts 9:1–8). That was exactly what God wanted him to do—never forget. When He breaks onto the scene, our lives are changed. We may feel as though we cannot take another step forward, but once we know that He is aware of what we are facing, the next step and the ones that follow become much easier. The conquest of Jericho became a reachable goal after Joshua got up and walked away from being with the angel of the Lord. The memory of the burning bush glowed in Moses' heart as he told Pharaoh, "The LORD, the God of the Hebrews, sent me to you, saying, 'Let My people go'" (Ex. 7:16).

Your situation may be a daunting challenge. Perhaps God has led you to a point where you know that you are on the right track, but you do not know how or when the door before you will open. Could it be that He wants to whisper to you, *Trust Me. Don't give up. Keep your eyes focused on Me and I will do exactly what I have promised to do at the right moment?* Panic swept through the hearts of the disciples as they crossed the Sea of Galilee at night. Calm seas had turned fierce. Gale-force winds blew across the water, and Jesus' followers were sure they were going to drown. As they fought to keep their boat afloat, someone saw what he thought was a ghost walking toward them. They had come face-to-face with circumstances that they could not explain or control, and they felt powerless. There was no way out. Then Jesus spoke to them, calming their hearts and dispelling their fears: "'Take courage; it is I, do not be afraid.' Then He got into the boat with them, and the wind stopped; and they were utterly astonished" (Mark 6:50–51).

God doesn't do anything casually, accidentally, or out of step with His timing and plan for our lives. He is never late, and He is never early. He always is on time, and He is sovereign over all things. The wind and waves were subject to His control. The city walls of Jericho could not withstand His might. Words spoken by Him can bring earthly rulers to their knees. He is not distant; He is completely involved with His creation. He knows all there is to know about the past, the present, and the future. He has chosen to love us with an unconditional love that is infinite in nature. Nothing on the earth or in heaven is greater than God's care for you.

Therefore, when He shows up in your life, never dismiss His coming as something ordinary or coincidental because it is not. I remember on one occasion that I needed to hear from Him; I was desperate for Him to confirm to me that what I was doing was correct. Everything within me said, "Go in the opposite direction. This way is not logical. It isn't the right thing to do. The timing is ridiculous." Then one night as I was on my knees praying, I had an awesome visitation from God. This type of thing does not happen often. But when it does, I want to be ready to do whatever He instructs me to do. That night, He made His message to me crystal clear. He had a certain way for me to go, and I needed to lay aside all human reasoning and do what He was telling me to do. Over the years, I have discovered that there are several principles involved with God's surprise visits.

First, He is willing to make His will known to us. He doesn't want us to make a mistake or to feel as though we have to guess between right and wrong. If we are patient and willing to wait and listen, we will know exactly what to do and how to do it. I believe that for many people, disappointment is a transition point to blessing. The way they view and handle the hurt or failure determines the outcome. If they angrily accuse God and become bitter, more than likely they are not going to have a sense of joy or blessing residing within their hearts. If they handle their hurt by turning to the Lord, seeking His insight, and being committed to following Him no matter how painful the future may appear, God will pour out His blessings on their lives. He wants to give good things—peace, security, stability, and hope—to all who love Him. No one is excluded except those who choose to turn away from Him.

Second, you should never underestimate what the Lord will do in your life. I have said this several times and probably will continue because it is a key to understanding the ways of God: He always has a plan, and He always has a purpose. When adversity strikes, you may not have time to think, *Lord, what is happening here?* However, after the immediate emergency passes, you will want to take time to ask Him to encourage your heart and show you, if possible, His will. He may give you the whole picture, or He may give you just enough for the moment. I remember hearing a story of a missionary leading a group of children at night to the top of a mountain in India. The lantern she was carrying gave off only enough light to see a few feet in front of her. Yet it was enough light to illuminate any tree roots or rocks that may have caused her to stumble. That is all we need at times—enough to light our paths and remind us that we are right in step with Him.

Third, God knows the future will be difficult, so He will surprise and reassure you by speaking to your heart. Jesus told His disciples that after His death, He would send a Comforter to be with them. The same Comforter that He sent to them lives within everyone who has accepted Him as Savior and Lord. Christ knew the aftermath of His crucifixion was going to be a very frightening time. He realized His disciples would abandon Him and hide for fear that they, too, would be arrested, tried, and killed. But He also knew that when the fear rose to a fevered pitch, He would come to them speaking words that would instantly calm and reassure them of God's love and victory.

Fourth, nothing is more important than the Lord Jesus Christ. I have watched and listened as people have placed many things before God in their lives—children, relatives, friends, spouses, material possessions, jobs, and wealth. God wanted to make sure that Abraham's heart and life were completely devoted to Him. When He instructed Abraham to take Isaac to the mountain and offer him as a sacrifice, the Lord was checking the level of his devotion. He was going to use this man in a mighty way. But if Abraham's love was greater for his son than it was for God, He wanted to expose it. Of course, God knew what would happen, but Abraham did not. This set of circumstances surprised him and also gave God the opportunity to provide the right sacrifice for him to offer. It underscores the fact that nothing should hold greater importance in our lives than God.

Would the Lord visit you in a way that is overwhelming? Yes, if this is needed, He will break into your life and offer the hope you need to continue. Never underestimate Him or His interest in you. He wants you to enjoy the intimacy of His fellowship. Many people do not experience this because they are not looking for it. They rush through life, not anticipating God's love. He wants you to know Him above everything else. The most important person in your life is Jesus Christ. You may live your entire lifetime and never experience what I have just written about in these few pages. Does that make you less holy than the person who does? No. It is just that God has not chosen to do this in your life. If He does, does that make you more superior or important? Absolutely not. It just means that God makes choices for specific reasons, and the way He works in one person's life may not be the same in another. God's plan and purpose fit each of us individually. Yours are tailored to suit you and no one else.

Regardless of what happens here and now, I am convinced that one day there is going to be a surprise visit that will impact all of us, and that is when Jesus Christ returns. He promised to return for those who have placed their faith in Him as their personal Savior, and at the right time, He will do just that. You can't anticipate when He will show up; you can't manipulate His coming. You can't do anything to change it or prevent it or hurry it up. You just need to be ready, and one way you do this is by admitting if there is sin in your life and asking God to forgive you and then to give you the ability to turn away from it. Just as He has chosen to love and save you, you must decide to say no to sin and yes to a life that is committed only to Him. When you make that choice, you will experience a wonderful, unending sense of joy and peace. Your life will change, and you will be free to live fully in the reality of His blessings and care.

Chapter Seven

RIGHT ON TIME

Do you ever feel that God is late? Or that He has ignored you? You have watched Him working in the lives of others while your prayers seem to go unanswered. You catch yourself going through a catalog of thoughts as you wonder what would block Him from answering your cries for help or blessing. *Have I sinned against You, Lord? Did I forget to do something that You want me to do? Have I acted in pride or been hurtful toward another? What would motivate You to be so late, quiet, and uncaring?*

God is never late. He is always on time. He answers our prayers, but often He does this according to His schedule and not ours. In all my years in ministry, I don't recall hearing anyone say, "God is rushing and hurrying. He is so far out in front of me that I cannot keep up." Usually the pleas I hear sound something like this: "I have prayed and prayed, but it is as if God is not listening. Or if He is, He is being silent. I don't know what to do. I need an answer now. I can't wait any longer. He knows the situation I'm in. What is He doing?" I can tell you exactly what He is doing. He is waiting until the timing is right, and when it is, He will open the door, motivate you to move ahead, or give you the wisdom to make the right decision. Until that time, He wants you to remain where you are—prepared to go forward but also waiting for His next set of instructions.

The prophet Isaiah wrote,

> Oh, that You would rend the heavens and come down,
>
> That the mountains might quake at Your presence—
>
> As fire kindles the brushwood, as fire causes water to boil—
>
> To make Your name known to Your adversaries,
>
> That the nations may tremble at Your presence!
>
> When You did awesome things which we did not expect,
>
> You came down, the mountains quaked at Your presence.
>
> For from days of old they have not heard or perceived by ear,
>
> Nor has the eye seen a God besides You,
>
> Who acts in behalf of the one who waits for Him. (Isa. 64:1–4)

As we think about the ways of God and how He works in our lives, we also must consider the way He schedules events to happen. The prophet Isaiah was writing to God's people during a turbulent time in history. The Babylonian Empire was increasing in power while Judah was declining. Years of sin and personal rebellion against God had turned them away from doing what He had commanded them to do—worship only Him. Nevertheless, Isaiah, like most of the other prophets, talked about their future punishment but also prophesied their return to the Lord. In the verses noted above Isaiah recounted the greatness of God and His ability to perform deeds that man cannot conceive.

God's ways are simply not our ways. He acts with a sense of purely profound holiness because He is holy and righteous. He knows all that has happened in the past, and He is completely aware of all that is up ahead. Nothing escapes His full attention. Much of what we read about Him is far too great for us to understand. We stand in awe of His power, and we wonder, *What motivates Him? Why does He do what He does? Why does He say what He does in Scripture? Who is this God that we worship? Can He love us when He knows that our hearts often wander away from Him?* Until you begin to understand His ways, you cannot understand the answer to these questions. Many people are not interested in knowing Him. They ignore Him and bypass every suggestion that would lead them into a personal relationship with the Savior of the world. As a result, they miss knowing Him and never have the opportunity to experience His greatest blessings.

Hell is a real destination for those who deny the love and forgiveness of Jesus Christ. Those who make a conscious choice to say no to His gift of salvation will reside there one day. I believe it is a place of torture and unimaginable emptiness and sorrow because of one primary thing: the absence of God. His presence will not be there. There will be other hideous ways to suffer in hell's dark chambers, but I cannot imagine the depth of agony those people will feel because they will have an awareness of what they will never be able to obtain. There is an appointed time for us to meet the Savior, and everyone will do this. No one will be able to escape, ignore, or dismiss it.

Walking in Step with God

God's schedule is based on His priorities and timing. And although I may not know what all of these include, I do know what is number one in His mind, and that is for you to have an intimate relationship with Him. It does not make any difference how much you serve Him, how much you give to Him, or how much you talk about Him. The most important thing to God is your personal relationship with Him. Therefore, He will govern and guide your schedule in a way that will bring you into an even closer relationship with Him. This may include doing things in your life that you do not like or enjoy. Some of what you experience will not be fun. In fact, there will be times when life feels painful and full of heartache, disappointment, and discouragement. You may suffer rejection and isolation. But there will also be times when you experience an awesome sense of pleasure, indescribable goodness, mercy, and kindness. The love and care of God will be evident.

The one thing you cannot forget—whether your circumstances are dark and stormy or bright and sunny—is that God is always at work. He is involved in every single moment of every day. However, there will be times when you are not on His schedule or in line with His will. You may drift into rebellion and disobedience. Or you may just say, "I'm not interested in God's schedule or His timing." But if you are truly committed to the Lord, you will learn to walk in step with His will. Then the doors that open before you and the opportunities He gives will take place within His perfect timing.

Sometimes you may think He is moving so slowly that it won't matter—just this once—if you force the issue and do what you think is best. You may even tell Him, "Lord, I can't wait another moment! Why are You holding me back?" The answer is simple, but it may not be that easy for you to accept: He knows what is ahead, and while the opportunity that you feel should take place today may look like a good one, it may not be His best. Remember, your goal always needs to be set on receiving what He has for you and not what you can drum up on your own. As I have said before, often His schedule is not ours. If we are committed to getting His best, then we will work in harmony with Him. His knowledge of our lives, needs, and future is infinite. He is omniscient and knows the best plan for us to take.

We do not have the ability to see into the future the way He does. He knows whether it is wise for us to follow through on our plans or to wait. Recently a member of my church explained her need for a new car. The one she was currently driving was older, but it was in fairly good condition. I understood that her desire was to feel safe while traveling to work and home. Because the car was almost ten years old, I did not feel she was being wasteful or unreasonable. Yet when she spoke of purchasing a new car, I felt the Lord saying, *Tell her to wait.* I asked her to consider waiting a little longer, even though she told of the good deal that she had been offered by the car dealership. I continued to sense the need for her to wait. She even explained how she could easily make the monthly payment, but that did not change what I felt inside. It was as if God was saying, *I have something better, and I need her to be patient.*

When we feel pushed to make a quick decision, we need to stop and ask God to confirm His will for us. He has a plan, and He will reveal it to us. The timing may not be right because there could be something better coming our way. After listening for several minutes, I told her that I understood that she had a true need in her life. However, I wanted to make a suggestion, and it was for her to trust God by laying the entire matter before Him in prayer and being committed to wait a little longer to see what the Lord would do. It was difficult, but she made a commitment to follow through on my suggestion. And a few weeks later, she came back to talk with me. I knew the moment that I saw her that God had not only answered her prayers, but He had blessed her in a far greater way. That was exactly what had happened. God provided a car that was far better than the one she originally wanted to purchase and for a much better price!

There will be times when we can sense the Lord instructing us to move forward. When He does, we need to pull up our tent pegs, pack, and follow Him, just as Abraham did. There will be other times when what we want to do just does not feel quite right. Something will be amiss, and we may not know what it is. And the truth is: when God is in control of our lives, all that we need to be concerned with is what He has given us to do. If that involves staying put, then we need to stay put. If it means going forward to a place that is unfamiliar, then we should follow Him there, knowing that wherever He leads, He will be there with us. We need to make a commitment to be on His schedule and not our own.

You should consider getting in step with God's plan and His schedule for three reasons:

1. *He is all-knowing.* I said earlier that He knows everything, but I want to add another thought that should help you understand why being on His schedule is so vital. He loves you with an everlasting love. Nothing is more important to Him than you. Now you may think, *That can't be right. What about the Middle East? Isn't that region much more important than I am?* No. Because He is omniscient, infinite in nature, and omnipotent, He can easily be in control of all the concerns of the world and still be completely aware of your every need and desire. How does He do this? He is God, and He lives through the presence of His Spirit in the lives of those who have accepted God's Son by faith as their personal Savior. Even if a person has not professed her faith in Him, He still knows her, her future, and her destiny. He is omniscient; He doesn't have to check His notes to see if He got something right. He has all the facts. Nothing happens outside His full knowledge.

When the enemy tempts us to think that God is not aware of our circumstances, we need to ignore his evil suggestions because it is not true. God is keenly aware of and interested in all that concerns us. When we make decisions based on the opinions of others, we are acting on partial knowledge and information. We also have to be careful that as we ask friends and family members to pray for us, we do not sway their opinions of the situation in our direction. Most of us know how to get a favorable response from others, but it is God's answer that you need the most. It is foolish to ignore Him under any circumstances and extremely unwise to push ahead when He wants us to wait.

2. *He is all-wise.* Realizing the depth of God's wisdom and then asking Him to lead you to the place you need to be are smart moves. You may have to put aside the words of others that would prompt you to move before the timing is right. Most of us want to move quickly when we need to ask God to show us when to step out, when to go forward slowly, and

when to move quickly and decisively. There is no way to fail when you know you are walking in step with God's plan. At this point someone may say, "But I don't feel as though God is speaking to me." He has promised in His Word to reveal Himself to us, but we must be still enough to hear Him. Reading and studying His principles train us to listen for His voice and teach us to watch for His open door of opportunity.

When your mind is overrun with thoughts and feelings of anxiety or fear, you won't be able to hear God clearly. Or if you do, you will question whether it is God or your own thoughts. Getting alone with Him on your knees in prayer is the first step to gaining the insight you need at every turn in life. Don't allow a pressured situation to compel you to act a certain way when you always have a choice. If you will seek Him, the Lord will give you the wisdom to make the right decision. He knows how to save you from a serious accident. He knows what it will take to heal your body when you are sick. And He knows what you need to say when you are witnessing to another person who does not personally know Him. Therefore, let go and let Him guide you. You can trust Him because all that we know and all that we have or will have and experience in the future is held within His righteous right hand. And He never fails.

3. *He is all-loving.* God's care for us is not based on anything we do or do not do. He loves us unconditionally. Regardless of what you have done in the past or will do in the future, His love for you will not change because He is unchangeable. He is the same yesterday, today, and forever. He does not and cannot change His mind because He is faithful, steady, and has perfect knowledge.

Think about this: our awesome God has a plan and a purpose for your life. It is not one of calamity or fear, though it may contain sorrow and suffering. We live in a fallen world. But even in times of extreme disappointment, sickness, and injury God is with you—sustaining you and seeking to encourage and lift you up. I have heard people cry out in frustration and disappointment wondering why God has allowed them to face extreme heartache. It always seems odd to me that we never throw up our hands and ask *why* when we are experiencing His joy and blessings.

Faced with an unspeakable loss, Job said,

> Naked I came from my mother's womb,
> And naked I shall return there.
> The LORD gave and the LORD has taken away.
> Blessed be the name of the LORD. (Job 1:21)

In chapter 2, he asked, "Shall we indeed accept good from God and not accept adversity?" (v. 10). It may be hard for you to accept, but God is acting in love even when He allows heartache to touch you. His plan is not for you to go through life never having a need or want or disappointment. Instead, it is for you to learn one primary truth from which everything else flows: God loves you. He acts in love toward you when you experience joy, hope, and the gratitude of others. Likewise, He loves you when you come up against difficulties.

I often remind people of Psalm 23. David had God's promises hidden within his heart. He was certain that once he was the anointed king of Israel, the next thing that would happen would be his move into the palace. But that did not happen. God gave him a promise, and then He began to train David how to rule as king. His preparation included walks through very dark emotional valleys—times when he was sure that he would never sit upon Israel's throne, and other times when he sensed God's favor and blessing.

Some things you and I experience will not feel very good. Like Mary and Martha in the aftermath of their brother's death, we will wonder why Jesus did not come quickly. But we also can come to the conclusion that Martha reached when she said, "Lord, if you had been here, my brother would not have died. Even now I know that whatever You ask of God, God will give You" (John 11:21–22). God had a greater plan in mind. He was going to raise their brother from the dead. If we had been in Martha's and Mary's place, could we accept Christ's decision to arrive later rather than on time by human standards?

God's schedule is the only one that is important. From our perspective, a certain plan may seem appropriate, but God sees it differently. He knows what He will accomplish in and through our lives. He had something far greater in store for this family, but they had to trust Him completely in the process. The issue usually involves the human desire to be in control. But if we're in control, then we won't readily accept the fact that God is. Therefore, we must decide whether to surrender to Him or continue striving to have something that was never ours in the first place. Control over all things belongs to God and not to us. He has given us the ability to make decisions, but in order for us ultimately to be successful and receive His blessings, we must follow His plan and schedule. Many people would rather try to manipulate their circumstances than allow God, who is all-loving, all-wise, and all-knowing, to give directions and guidance.

He knows that it takes time for us to understand this. Mary and Martha could not comprehend what the Lord was doing. However, once they saw their brother walk away from the grave, their minds were changed, and they knew that Someone far greater was in control of their lives. It takes patience to allow God the space and time to work in our lives. For example, we may have a problem, and because we do not see anything happening, we start to think that He is being slow or does not care what is taking place.

When I was young, my mother decided that we would plant a vegetable garden. She wanted me to learn how plants grow. We dug up an area in our backyard and planted some seeds in nice, neat rows. Although I don't remember the type of seed, I do remember being excited. She told me that we would cover them up, water them, and wait for the results. "It won't be long, Charles," she said with a smile, "before you will notice a few green sprouts pushing up through the dirt. When you see these, you will know that the plants are growing." Every day or so I walked out into our yard and checked for any changes. There were none.

After several days and no action, I became impatient. A week went by and still nothing happened. Waiting can be difficult for a young person. It also can be difficult for many of us who are much older. But there is a way for us to wait and not become impatient. After I had waited for what seemed to be a sufficient amount of time, I decided to see what the problem was. Mother was at work, and I went out to the garden and began digging. In fact, I dug up the whole thing! Years later, I reminded her of our garden experiment, and she laughed and said, "I forgot to tell you that it takes time for the seed to grow."

I expected immediate results, and when I did not get them, I took matters into my own hands. What I want you to realize is that I did not gain anything from being impatient. Our garden was ruined, and we had to start over. Often, this scenario is repeated in our personal lives when we refuse to wait. God begins to work, but we want things to happen quickly. We have a timetable, but it does not line up with His. We forget that most of God's choice servants waited for Him to work in their lives. David waited years before he became king over Israel. Joseph faced a similar test of faith. But those men were not alone. The prophets foretold the Messiah's coming, but they did not see His coming in their lifetimes. God had not forgotten; He had a plan, and they simply accepted it.

One reason we think God is working slowly is that we have our own agendas. We are taught to plan and to organize our lives for specific purposes, but many people do not know God's will. Others who do know find it hard to wait. An important lesson you can learn concerning God's schedule is that He has a perfect sense of timing. He does not act randomly but instead has a specific purpose in mind.

One woman who does not attend my church explained her sense of unfulfillment. She received a paycheck twice a month. After it was deposited, she headed to the mall to start spending almost all of it, except what was essential to pay her bills. I asked her three questions:

"What is your purpose in life?"

"What are your goals for the future?"

"Have you asked God to reveal His plan for your life to you?"

She could not answer any of them and was stunned to learn that God actually cared what she did with her time and her life. "I want to be happy," she said.

"What does happiness mean to you?" I prodded.

She did not hesitate to respond, "Having plenty of money."

"But what happens if you lose all that you have?" It is hard to believe that she had not thought of this, especially in our day and time when changes in jobs and lifestyles can come quickly.

She was silent for a moment and then replied, "I'll find a way to make it."

But most people don't. This type of self-determination apart from God lands us in deep trouble. Instead of our pulling in the opposite direction, He wants us to walk with Him in fellowship and unity, desiring His will for our lives. His love for us is so great that He actually enjoys being with us, teaching us His ways, and watching us grow in our awareness of Him. But when we refuse, we are the ones who suffer. This woman was living for the moment, and even though she believed she was making her own decisions, she was actually bound to the fact that she did not have a real plan for the future and no schedule other than to live from paycheck to paycheck.

People who become frozen in their thinking rarely know how to look beyond their immediate need. They cannot visualize the broad scope of the blessings that God has for them. They falsely assume that they are the freest when they make their plans apart from Him or anyone else who seeks to provide guidance. But they are not free. True freedom comes from working with a winning strategy, following a plan, setting godly goals, and allowing

Him to show you what is best. Lasting freedom comes through surrender to holy God, who loves you and knows exactly how to use to the fullest the talents and gifts He has given you. When we make His agenda ours, we plot a course toward success and fulfillment. There is no way to miss His blessings when we are committed to His plan. Peter wisely stated, "The Lord is not slow about His promise" (2 Peter 3:9).

In God's mind, a year is nothing. Time is not a concern to Him. He is aware of having the right timing in place, but He is in control of every second. Therefore, He can set up an event or alter a schedule without our noticing the change. He spoke this world into existence:

> In the beginning God created the heavens and the earth. The earth was formless and void, and darkness was over the surface of the deep, and the Spirit of God was moving over the surface of the waters. Then God said, "Let there be light"; and there was light. God saw that the light was good; and God separated the light from the darkness. God called the light day, and the darkness He called night. And there was evening and there was morning, one day. Then God said, "Let there be an expanse in the midst of the waters, and let it separate the waters from the waters." . . . Then God said, "Let the waters below the heavens be gathered into one place, and let the dry land appear"; and it was so. (Gen. 1:1–6, 9)

The power of God is limitless. He cannot be contained or reduced to human actions. He is above all things, and He knows exactly what will happen next, how it will take place, and what He will do in the aftermath.

Living According to God's Timetable

Our challenge is really not a challenge at all, at least not to God. We encounter pressure and stress when we want to see something take place and believe it is a part of His will for our lives, but nothing happens. I remember listening to a young man that I met through a friend. His sole interest was to make a difference in our world. He had so many ideas that it was hard to listen and not feel compelled to join in on his conversation. Immediately after college, he accepted a nice job with a corporation that provided room for him to grow. But after several months on the job, he observed those in senior-level positions and wondered why he had to wait to compete with them. He felt he had been given a strong set of communication skills and the raw talent to make things happen, but he remained on the same level. There will be seasons in our lives when God wants us to wait and to rest in the fact that even though we do not see the evidence of His work, He is on the move. Joseph waited years for God's deliverance. David had to wait to assume the throne of Israel. Mary and Martha waited for Jesus' arrival in Bethany after their brother had died. Any time God calls us to be still and wait, we can be certain that He is going to do something absolutely fantastic.

When He tells us He is going to work in a certain area, we can be sure that He will. The question we need to answer is, "How do we wait for His will to be revealed?"

We Wait in Faith

Because we know He is in control of all things and has the power to protect and keep us safe even in the most trying circumstances, we can trust Him to do what is best. Just because there are times when we do not see the physical evidence of His work does not mean that God is inactive. At the close of a Sunday morning service, a lady came forward and told me, "I have prayed and prayed and prayed, and nothing has happened." I asked her whether she was fully committed to trusting God, even if it meant that her prayers were not answered. This woman agreed that she would wait on the Lord and allow Him to give her His best, though it might come in a different package than the one she expected.

We have perfect faith when we trust Him because we know that what He has said, He will do. A lack of faith will prevent us from gaining the wisdom we need to know Him and to understand His ways. It takes faith—perfect faith—to live and walk each day in unhindered fellowship with Jesus Christ.

We Wait with Patience

There are two requirements for gaining God's best. First, we must have a heart and life totally yielded to Him. Second, we need to realize that we cannot hurry God. At times, I have told Him that I could not wait another moment. I felt as though I had to have an answer, but my emergency was not valid. The pressures of our world have no effect on Him or His timetable. He is God, and every single time I felt pushed to make a decision that was not God-directed, I could sense Him cautioning me to wait. Sometimes, I discovered later the reason why I needed to be still, patient, and open to His suggestions. Usually He had something much better in store for me. Other times, I never learned why I had to wait for His answer. But I can say without a doubt that one of the greatest lessons of maturity is learning to be patient.

We Wait with Hope

If you believe that God does not hear your prayers and is not going to work in your life, more than likely you will miss His coming—the times He draws near and makes His closeness known to you. You also will run the risk of ignoring His guidance. People who doubt His goodness miss out on so much. Satan whispers words of defeat. And if we buy into his lies, we run the risk of getting off track and out of step with God. Hope in His eternal love for us is the unbreakable, undeniable truth that keeps us steady in the midst of every storm.

The disciples panicked on the Sea of Galilee when storm winds rose and a swelling sea threatened to engulf their boat. They looked out over the water and saw a figure walking toward them. As mentioned earlier, they thought it was a ghost. Why did they fail to see Jesus? This was the lesson He wanted them to learn: "I am beside you in every circumstance. Nothing is too great for Me to handle. I'm never surprised, shocked, or dismayed. I am the One who is in control of the wind, the rain, every aspect of the weather, and I hold your life within My hand. I will not let you go." When they realized that it was Jesus and not some horrid phantom, their level of anxiety dropped. He commanded the wind to stop blowing, and it responded. He spoke to the waves, and they obeyed Him. What false god has this same ability? There is none like Him.

Having the Right Perspective

You may be tempted to think, *I just wish I could have known that certain things were going to happen.* You can never know everything. First, you do not have the ability to deal with the problems that come your way or even, in many cases, the joys that God offers you. Second, if you want to feel as though you have a greater degree of control, try surrendering all that you have and all that you want to be to God. It is amazing that when we let go—just trust Him—we begin to experience a fresh sense of hope. Instead of going from one cloudy situation to another, we begin to look at life with an optimistic attitude.

There was a dear lady on our In Touch staff for years. Everyone who knew her loved her. Even when she was acting a little feisty, there was still a twinkle in her eye that let you know one thing: Jesus was in control of her life. Later in life when she found out that she had cancer and would not live much longer, she continued to bring joy to all who talked with her. Yes, she was tired and openly admitted that her body was wearing down. By earthly standards, she was not wealthy, but from God's perspective she was rich beyond anything this world has known because she had an eternal hope living within her. She also had the right perspective. Her thoughts were set on Jesus Christ and not her circumstances. Her hope was eternal and could not be dashed by impending death.

If the source of your hope is based on earthly treasures, then you are going to experience one disappointment after another. If your hope is not based on God moving on your behalf—proving again and again that He loves you—then you will battle discouragement. Remember He told Moses to tell them that I AM was sending him. The circumstances of life do not change God. He is eternally the same. And whether you achieve great victories or ones that are small and barely mentioned is not the issue. The author of Proverbs wrote, "Know that wisdom is thus for your soul; if you find it, then there will be a future, and your hope will not be cut off" (24:14).

The apostle Paul reminded us that when we wait on God and live according to His schedule, we will have hope. Paul also had the right perspective. He was tuned to God's schedule and not to his own, saying, "We also exult in our tribulations, knowing that tribulation brings about perseverance; and perseverance, proven character; and proven character, hope; and hope does not disappoint, because the love of God has been poured out within our hearts through the Holy Spirit who was given to us" (Rom. 5:3–5).

Even though David was anointed at sixteen to be king, he did not take the throne until he was thirty years old. God spent all those years preparing him for the job that he would do one day. We may think, *It is just taking too long.* But it's not according to God's timetable. He knows what is involved in our preparation, and He is committed to training us for the task He has given us to do. Not only did God take years to prepare David, but He also allowed him to face deep disappointment, rejection, fear, anxiety, and betrayal.

There is only one way that we are trained to live this life, and it is through experience and faith in Jesus Christ. There have been times when I did something and later thought, *I could have done that better,* or *If I had said something differently, it would have turned out better.* We will continue to learn more about God and His ways until we go to be with Him. The spiritual maturation process never stops because there is no way for us to know God fully and completely. This idea is exciting because it means that we will spend a lifetime getting to know Him and allowing Him to train us for service here and for when we are with Him in heaven.

Understanding God's Schedule

Paul sometimes had to wait on God's timing. He knew the Lord wanted him to go to Rome and preach the gospel, but he was not given the freedom to go until the timing was right. On another occasion, the apostle believed that he needed to take his missionary movement into Asia Minor, but God's Spirit would not allow that move:

> They passed through the Phrygian and Galatian region, having been forbidden by the Holy Spirit to speak the word in Asia; and after they came to Mysia, they were trying to go into Bithynia, and the Spirit of Jesus did not permit them; and passing by Mysia, they came down to Troas. A vision appeared to Paul in the night: a man of Macedonia was standing and appealing to him, and saying, "Come over to Macedonia and help us." When he had seen the vision, immediately we sought to go into Macedonia, concluding that God had called us to preach the gospel to them. So putting out to sea from Troas, we ran a straight course to Samothrace, and on the day following to Neapolis. (Acts 16:6–11)

I'm sure Paul knew there was a great need for the gospel to be preached in Asia. He knew that few had heard the truth of the gospel, but something was not right. He tried to enter the region, but the Holy Spirit stopped him. He tried again at another point, but once more, the Lord's answer was no. Finally he submitted to God's plan and went into Macedonia. We know that was when he met Luke and found great solace in his company. In fact, some of Paul's strongest churches were established in this region.

Later, when the timing was right, God allowed the message of His grace and unconditional love to be preached through Asia. If Paul had not listened to the Lord and agreed to get in step with His schedule, he would have faced trouble as a result of his disobedience. He also would have experienced a reduction in power. God empowers us to do His will, but He is not obligated to bless anything that we decide we are going to do on our own. Training requires total commitment, and it means adhering to a schedule. Runners do not win marathons apart from discipline. They must train, and they must have a strict schedule.

Over the years, I have counseled many young couples who felt as though they "must" get married. Sometimes, the older people become, the more they will be tempted to think they will never meet the right person to marry. When they do meet someone, one of the first things they think is, *Wonder what type of spouse he or she would make?* But in actuality, their first thought should be to get to know the person—his or her devotion to God and moral values. The question needs to be asked, "Lord, is this the right one for me?" Then you can consider whether the person shares your interests and whether there is mutual attraction. I've witnessed a lot of disappointment and heartache in this area because people want to rush into a long-term commitment without taking time to know whether the individual is God's best. For many, the tendency to "act now and ask questions later" can lead to only one conclusion—deep regret.

If you feel as though you are being pushed to make a decision, then you need to stop and ask God to give you His timetable. Remember, He is never in a hurry. Jesus did not rush from one place to another. He knew His schedule and kept every single appointment without becoming frantic or overwhelmed. He may show you that what you are about to do is not His best for your life. Or He may make it perfectly clear that you are in the center of His will, and therefore, you can go forward.

If you are pushing to gain some advantage or answer to prayer on your own, then you could be in dangerous territory. Also, Christians need to be careful about encouraging people to go ahead, slow down, or wait apart from spending time with the Lord in prayer. Most of us love to attend weddings. They are happy times when we get to share the joy and love that others are experiencing. But none of that justifies our desire to push someone else into a relationship that could turn out badly. You can certainly introduce two people to each other and pray for them. But God needs to be the One who gives them the encouragement to get married or to wait.

We can, and should on occasion, ask the advice of others. There is wisdom in seeking the counsel of others. However, the final decision about any matter needs to come as a result of being with the Lord in prayer. He may ask you to wait indefinitely. Or He may allow everything to fall into place in a very short time. Most people who have been talked into a decision usually end up regretting the fact that they listened to "well-meaning" friends. If you will set a goal to do exactly as God leads you to do, then you always will be in the center of His will. Our challenge is to surrender to His control and guidance.

Looking Forward with Hope

For this to happen, you need to come to a point where you accept God's sovereignty. Once you do, you will begin to understand the goodness that He has in mind for your life. Though the nation of Israel had been taken into captivity, Jeremiah had a tremendous sense of hope as he wrote,

> This I recall to my mind,
> Therefore I have hope.
> The LORD's lovingkindnesses indeed never cease,
> For His compassions never fail. They are new every morning;
> Great is Your faithfulness.
> "The LORD is my portion," says my soul,

"Therefore I have hope in Him."

The LORD is good to those who wait for Him,

To the person who seeks Him. (Lam. 3:21–25)

When you live in sync with God's plan, you will have fresh hope and encouragement. The prophet Jeremiah had the dismal task of telling the people of Judah that because of their sin, they would be taken into captivity. However, the Lord also had given Jeremiah a promise: one day Judah and Israel would return to Jerusalem. Their captivity would come to an end, and a remnant would return to the city (Jer. 30).

The prophet could have asked God to give him a specific date and time for the scheduled return, but he didn't. He could have become angry and bitter over the pain that he knew the people would experience as a result of their sin, but he would not do it. Though we read of his deep distress in Lamentations and in the book that bears his name, Jeremiah trusted God. He did not experience immediate relief. In fact, he went days and months and years without any noticeable change in his situation. The truth is: his situation grew worse while he was imprisoned. Yet he kept his focus on God. Though captivity was painful, he knew that at the right time, God would do exactly what He promised. Babylon would be judged for its sins against Israel and Judah (Jer. 51), and they would be restored. The people would not be cast off but would return home.

Are you able to look beyond your present circumstance and see God's faithfulness at work? Understanding His ways and how He works in your life always leads to hope. In Psalm 27, David proclaimed,

The LORD is my light and my salvation;

Whom shall I fear?

The LORD is the defense of my life;

Whom shall I dread?

When evildoers came upon me to devour my flesh,

My adversaries and my enemies, they stumbled and fell.

Though a host encamp against me,

My heart will not fear;

Though war arise against me,

In spite of this I shall be confident. (vv. 1–3)

This psalm is a prayer of confident confession. David was embattled with threats from his enemies, but a single truth fueled his optimism: he knew that God was his ultimate protection. But this principle was not something he immediately understood. It took years for David to learn this truth. God trained him to live with this reality in mind through the heartaches and disappointments he suffered. David experienced periods of great want and distress. He knew God had anointed him king of Israel, but any outward evidence of this becoming a reality had faded. Years spent running from a jealous king had enticed him to wonder, *How long, Lord?*

What would you have done if you were in David's position? Would you be able to view your present situation and write these words he wrote in Psalm 27?

Teach me Your way, O Lord,

And lead me in a level path

Because of my foes.

Do not deliver me over to the desire of my adversaries,

For false witnesses have risen against me,

And such as breathe out violence.

I would have despaired unless I had

    believed that I would see the goodness of the Lord

In the land of the living.

Wait for the Lord;

Be strong and let your heart take courage;

Yes, wait for the Lord. (vv. 11–14)

If David had owned a watch, it would have been set to God's timetable and not his own. But he did not get to this point quickly. It takes time to understand God's ways. Therefore, ask Him to help you set timely goals for your life and become a person who waits for His best rather than one who rushes forward too quickly or hangs back when He has made the blessing available. Always remember, the time you spend waiting can be some of the dearest time you will spend with the Lord. Why? Because you are surrendering to His will and you also are saying:

- "Lord, I know You are sovereign, and I want to obey You."
- "I realize You have Your best for me, and You will provide it at the right time."
- "Lord, I possibly could get what I want, but I realize I would not enjoy it apart from Your blessing and affirmation."

Making the Best Choice

What do you do if you have made the wrong choice, moved ahead of God, and become involved in something that is not His best?

Once you realize you are no longer operating according to His schedule, admit what you have done to Him. After being confronted about his sin with Bathsheba, David immediately turned to the Lord and prayed,

Against You, You only, I have sinned

And done what is evil in Your sight,

So that You are justified when You speak

And blameless when You judge. (Ps. 51:4)

Seek His restoration because it is available to you. David did not stop with a confession. He understood something about God's ways, and he knew from all he had learned, witnessed, and read that the Lord would restore him if he truly repented. He added,

> Create in me a clean heart, O God,
> And renew a steadfast spirit within me.
> Do not cast me away from Your presence
> And do not take Your Holy Spirit from me.
> Restore to me the joy of Your salvation
> And sustain me with a willing spirit. (vv. 10–12)

Notice there is no hint of giving up on life. I have heard believers who fail miserably say, "I just can't do this. I'm never going to learn what I need to learn. I've failed again, and I'll never get over it." Yes, you will with God's help.

Move forward by trusting God for your future. David gave us a key insight into his love of and faith in God: "Then I will teach transgressors Your ways, and sinners will be converted to You" (v. 13). The entire time he was confessing his sin, he was thinking, *Lord, help me to understand what I have done. I was wrong—horribly wrong. I know that You are going to deal with this sin, but I also want to learn from this experience so that I will never do it again. Then I will tell others where I have failed and how they can avoid doing the same thing.* What was David's focus? God and God alone. When you yield to temptation and sin against God, what do you think of first? Do you wonder who else knows and whether you will be embarrassed, or do you think of what you have done and how it has hurt your fellowship with God, who loves you more than words can express?

When you live in tune with God's schedule, you will not be prone to fret and worry. The psalmist reminded us to "rest in the Lord and wait patiently for Him" (Ps. 37:7). Why can you wait? You can rest and wait in God's care because He is omnipotent and all that you need is found in Him. If there is a need for an answer to a problem, He has it. If there is a deficiency, He knows exactly how and when to bring the increase. If there is trouble, heartache, sorrow, or the desire to have a need met, He knows all about it and is committed to answering when you trust Him. He does not ignore your legitimate needs. He also provides many of your desires, especially the ones that honor Him.

How should you wait for His timing to unfold? The psalmist told us to wait in silence with a trusting heart:

> My soul waits in silence for God only;
> From Him is my salvation,
> He only is my rock and my salvation.
> My stronghold; I shall not be greatly shaken. (Ps. 62:1–2)

It takes courage to walk through difficult times with God. Many times, you can't see what is coming in the future, but you know something is about to change. God knows how to prepare you for the future. You may say, "God, I can't handle this anymore." But He can and He does when you confess your faith in Him. Then like Job, you will experience new blessings and fresh hope.

A few years ago, I was asked to speak to a group of businessmen while I was in New Zealand. The pastor who issued the invitation forgot to tell me that I would be speaking eight times. We started at 8:30 a.m., and I spoke for thirty minutes. Then I walked back to an area to rest for a few minutes before doing the same thing all over again. The area where I rested was cold. The floor was concrete, and there was nothing in the room. I recalled a passage of Scripture that God had placed in my mind earlier that day. I opened my Bible and read it again, then closed it and lay down on the floor in prayer. I put the

Bible under my head, and I prayed, "God, here is what You promised. You said, 'Those who wait for the LORD will gain new strength; they will mount up with wings like eagles, they will run and not get tired, they will walk and not become weary' [Isa. 40:31]. You promised that if I would wait for You, then You would renew my energy; and Your might, power, and anointing would be mine. I can't do this in my own strength. I'm waiting for You to help me." What do you think the Lord did? Exactly what He promised to do. I preached eight times, and when I finished the last time, I thought about my prayer and realized I wasn't even tired! Have you ever watched an eagle fly? They are powerful, accurate, and extremely strong.

Something happens when you and I get on God's schedule. His blessings begin to flow our way, and we can travel much farther and endure greater obstacles because we are operating not in our strength but in God's. And that is the primary difference between failure and success in the Christian life.

Chapter Eight

GOD USES ADVERSITY

No one enjoys pain—physical or emotional. But there is a way to handle it better, and it is through understanding the way God works and why He does what He does. Remember the request that Moses prayed? It was the one I used in the opening of this book. He prayed, "[Lord,] if I have found favor in Your sight, let me know Your ways that I may know You, so that I may find favor in Your sight" (Ex. 33:13). These words were not written during his commissioning in front of the burning bush. They were penned in the middle of the Exodus when the people had become unruly and were complaining loudly. The pressure on Moses had to be overwhelming. It is one thing to be the leader of a hundred people, but he had been given the task of leading some two million people to a new home—one that he did not know. Each day was a walk of faith. If he had been given a compass, it would have been of little use because God was the One who was leading him. Moments of extreme exhaustion and confusion are replaced by clarity and hope whenever we trust God and obey Him.

It does not matter whether you are suffering with a long-term illness or an emotional problem that has tempted you to wonder if there is any hope for your future. If you can believe this one principle, then you will be able to cross over to a land of promise and future just as Israel did. God has a plan and a purpose for your suffering. And the truth is, even if Moses had been given a textbook on the subject, he would not have learned what he needed to know apart from suffering.

It is in times of great distress that we gain extreme insight into God's faithfulness. Over the years, I have watched people struggle with adversity. Most of the time, their battle is not so much with the problem as it is with their desire to control the situation. They won't surrender it to God. Therefore, the battle only intensifies because He wants us to let go of our need to control our circumstances and trust Him. Most of us know what it feels like to be out of control. We want to "do something"—anything other than to be still. And yet many times this is exactly what He wants us to do—rest in His care, wait for His timing, and trust Him to work on our behalf.

Recently I began to battle what seemed to be a cold. Although it was nothing serious, I became tired easily and needed to rest more. While my doctor was not completely sure what I had, she was certain that the cure involved extra time off from my normal duties. Members of my staff and congregation know that extended time away from the pulpit is not something I deeply enjoy. I had just taken some time off and was ready to begin the new year with a full set of sermons. Nevertheless, the moment I heard my doctor's advice, I knew that was exactly what God wanted me to do. I never heard an audible voice speaking to me, but what my spirit did hear was this: *Trust Me. I know what I'm doing. You need to rest at this point in the journey.*

Everything within me wanted to keep going. It was the start of another year, and I also knew there were many new opportunities taking place through the ministry of In Touch. I never grow tired of being involved with preaching and teaching God's truth. But over the years, I have learned the importance of listening to God. In this case, God wanted to draw me aside to be alone with Him for a short season of prayer, reflection, and insight.

A couple of years ago I was in a remote location doing some photography. In fact, I was on the top of a very high mountain when all of a sudden my cell phone started to ring. I had forgotten to turn it off, and the thought struck me that there are very few times when we are alone and unconnected to the world around us. No wonder we have such a difficult time hearing the voice of God speaking to our hearts. And there is no doubt in my mind that He uses suffering to accomplish His will in our lives. As I have written in an earlier chapter, God allows adversity. He is not the author of evil, but He will use the trials we endure to teach us more about Himself and to build a level of intimacy between us and Him that is remarkable. Of course, we must be willing to listen, to be still, and to be open to His guidance and, at times, His conviction in the area of sin.

God Is Committed to Using Our Suffering

At some point each one of us will suffer illness or pain. I have suffered in far greater ways than having a simple cold. But there are people who have suffered individual hurt and physical trauma that I have never experienced. Yet because I have faced adversity, I can say without a doubt that no matter how deep our valleys may seem, God's love and care for us go infinitely deeper. We suffer for many reasons.

Suffering Can Be the Result of Sin

In Romans 12, the apostle Paul told us that we can live free of sin's captivating power through Jesus Christ. However, when we yield to temptation of any kind, we reap what we sow and are forced to deal with the consequences of our sinful choices. He wrote, "I urge you, brethren, by the mercies of God, to present your bodies a living and holy sacrifice, acceptable to God, which is your spiritual service of worship. And do not be conformed to this world, but be transformed by the renewing of your mind, so that you may prove what the will of God is, that which is good and acceptable and perfect" (Rom. 12:1–2). God wants us to say no to sin and to be trained for His service by doing the very things that lead to a closer relationship with Him. If sin is involved, we will not be able to do this. Our minds will be divided and our hearts drawn away by temptation. No matter how much we proclaim our love for God, we must do exactly what Jesus instructed the rich young ruler to do, and that was to leave everything behind that would cause him to stumble and to follow only Him.

Sin robs you of the rewards He has for you. Adultery carries a hefty price tag. Having sex outside marriage often leads to far-reaching pain that includes heartache, betrayal, and rejection. Even if you end up getting married, the scars that are left from going against God's principles can run deep. That was why Paul told us "not to let sin reign in your mortal body so that you obey its lusts, and do not go on presenting the members of your body to sin as instruments of unrighteousness; but present yourselves to God as those alive from the dead, and your members as instruments of righteousness to God" (Rom. 6:12–13). The spirit of gossip can ruin a relationship and cause others to doubt your commitment to the Lord. Outbursts of anger, resentment, and jealousy can and do undermine God's work in your life. You can turn away from sin, but you cannot do it alone. You must turn your life and every sinful habit over to Jesus Christ.

God Allows Suffering and Discipline Because He Loves Us

God is in the process of training us for service in His kingdom. He knows that we may not be where we need to be spiritually. Therefore, He stretches our faith and uses discipline to teach us how to stay the course and finish the race. If we give up too soon, we will never reach our full potential. The author of Hebrews urged,

> Let us run with endurance the race that is set before us, fixing our eyes on Jesus, the author and perfecter of faith, who for the joy set before Him

endured the cross, despising the shame, and has sat down at the right hand of the throne of God. For consider Him who has endured such hostility by sinners against Himself, so that you will not grow weary and lose heart. You have not yet resisted to the point of shedding blood in your striving against sin; and you have forgotten the exhortation which is addressed to you as sons,

"My son, do not regard lightly the discipline of the Lord,

Nor faint when you are reproved by Him;

For those whom the Lord loves He disciplines,

And He scourges every son whom He receives."

It is for discipline that you endure; God deals with you as with sons; for what son is there whom his father does not discipline? But if you are without discipline, of which all have become partakers, then you are illegitimate children and not sons. . . . All discipline for the moment seems not to be joyful, but sorrowful; yet to those who have been trained by it, afterwards it yields the peaceful fruit of righteousness. (12:1–8, 11)

We May Suffer Persecution as a Result of Our Faith in Christ

This concept is nothing new. Because of their faith in God, New Testament believers suffered severely at the hands of Nero and other Roman rulers. But throughout Israel's history, one nation after another took up fighting positions in an effort to eliminate God's people. In modern times, this has remained a sad but recurring theme. Satan's focus is set, and that is to destroy the church. He will use any form of attack in order to accomplish his goal. And he never gives up. He is a powerful foe, but his strength pales when compared to the infinite power and strength of almighty God. He knows how to lead you straight through a dangerous place. He can conceal, protect, and restore you, but the focus of your heart must be set on Him or you will try to help yourself and end up failing miserably. Fighting on your own behalf without God's strength and ability is totally exhausting.

God Allows Suffering when We Violate Good Health Principles

Eating right, resting at appropriate times, and exercising will prevent many health issues that are prevalent today. You may inherit a health problem, but you can lessen your chances of falling ill to it when you are doing what is right instead of ignoring the problem or living any way you please. Not long ago, a young pastor told me that his father died as a result of a heart attack. Other family members also had battled heart disease. Now that he was getting a little older he decided to work with his medical doctor to assure that he was living a healthy lifestyle, which included eating well, exercising almost every day, and keeping a close eye on his cholesterol level that had started to inch up. After several months, he was back in a healthy range and promised his wife and children that he would continue to do what was right. We make choices every day. We can learn to say no to sin, but then we also need to learn to say yes to healthy lifestyles and habits. When we do this, we don't suffer as often. This is not to say that some diseases are unavoidable. But even when we battle a terminal illness, we can ask God to help us live wisely.

God Uses Suffering to Gain Our Attention and Draw Us Closer to Himself

One of the smartest things we can do when adversity strikes is to ask, "Lord, show me what You want to teach me through this suffering." Peter wrote, "Beloved, do not be surprised at the fiery ordeal among you, which comes upon you for your testing, as though some strange thing were happening to you; but to the degree that you share the sufferings of Christ, keep on rejoicing, so that also at the revelation of His glory you may rejoice with exultation. If you are reviled for the name of Christ, you are blessed, because the Spirit of glory and of God rests on you" (1 Peter 4:12–14). Don't be shocked, don't be threatened, and don't give up. The enemy is going about doing what he has done since his fall from heaven, and he will continue until Jesus throws him into the lake of fire forever (Rev. 20:10).

Be assured that God is fully in control. Could He prevent tragedy?

Absolutely. Nevertheless, there are times when He allows suffering. Jesus prayed, "[Father,] I do not ask You to take them out of the world, but to keep them from the evil one. They are not of the world, even as I am not of the world. Sanctify them in the truth; Your word is truth. As You sent Me into the world, I also have sent them into the world" (John 17:15–18). Our spiritual address is located in heaven. It is our future home. Until God calls us to be with Him, though, we live an earthbound existence. For now, trouble, trial, and difficulty are parts of the Christian experience.

God Uses Adversity to Develop Our Personal Righteousness and Maturity

This is what the passage cited from 1 Peter is saying. The will of God for your life is that you would desire to live righteously and become a godly man or woman. He knows exactly what it will take to get you positioned to do this very thing. He also is aware that many times if He does not take drastic measures, you could easily keep going in a wrong direction and end up far from Him.

What really happens when you make a wrong choice? You step away from God's best; you miss His blessings; and you are no longer living within His will. I have seen God open doors of opportunities, and people choose not to go through them for one reason or another. Many times, they hesitate because of fear of the unknown. We should always ask God to make His way clear. He has a plan, and He will reveal this to you when you ask Him.

God Allows Suffering Because He Wants to Prune Us for His Service

John recorded these words of Jesus: "I am the true vine, and My Father is the vinedresser. Every branch in Me that does not bear fruit, He takes away; and every branch that bears fruit, He prunes it so that it may bear more fruit" (John 15:1–2). If a grapevine is not regularly pruned, it will not produce good fruit. You have to cut out the dead parts and anything that would hinder growth and productivity. When a tree is pruned, it may bleed sap. When

God begins to prune us, He looks for dead growth, checks for branches that are not going to produce fruit, and then goes to work. He may reveal an attitude that is not in keeping with His principles. Or He could expose a habit or action that is not becoming to who we are in Christ. His goal is for us to be righteous and godly. These are characteristics of His nature, and our lives should reflect the same things when we are living for Him.

At times, His pruning knife works deep within our lives, and we may feel as though it is extreme or that we will never recover. God knows exactly how much to remove so that our lives produce an abundance of fruit. In the pruning process, He may use times of suffering to maximize our potential. He allows difficulty so He can gain our full attention. When He does, He points out the things in our lives that are preventing us from being our best. This process does not happen quickly. It is ongoing and continues throughout our lives as he prunes away wrong attitudes, distractions, and habits that lead to ungodly character.

He Uses Severe Trials to Teach Us Obedience

When my children were young, they asked me why they needed to listen to me. Like most very young children, they had to learn the principle of obedience by experiencing the consequences that came from ignoring my instruction. When they were old enough to understand, I explained to them that obedience set the stage for the way they would live their lives for God. If they rebelled and refused to do what I told them, more than likely they would do the same later with the Lord. When they grew up, they would have trouble obeying others in positions of authority. When you do not teach your children about parental authority, you are essentially telling them that authority is not important. If they don't learn to obey you, they will have a very difficult time obeying God, and that involves more than saying, "Yes, sir," and "Yes, ma'am." All of us must understand that God has created a system of authority for our protection.

When He tells us to do something, we need to obey Him on the basis of who is doing the talking. Abraham obeyed God when the Lord said,

> Go forth from your country,
> And from your relatives
> And from your father's house,
> To the land which I will show you;
> And I will make you a great nation,
> And I will bless you. (Gen. 12:1–2)

The Lord did not give Abraham all the details about what was going to happen. The Lord just instructed him to pack up his tent and his family and leave his home. The most important thing that we, as believers, can do is to obey God. He gave Abraham a few details about the future, but there was not an outline about the future. Likewise, there will be times in our lives when God tells us simply to go forward by faith. He may or may not give us a list of details. "Trust Me" may be His only instruction. Abraham made the right choice. It was strictly one of obedience and trust, and this is exactly what God wanted him to do at this point in his life.

Are you willing to obey God no matter what His instructions include? Or do you try to reason and rationalize your way through a situation without considering His will? Many people have this view: *If God's plan fits my plan, then it must be right.* Abraham walked through his life in step with God, and so did Jesus Christ. The author of Hebrews told us that He learned obedience: "In the days of His flesh, He offered up both prayers and supplications with loud crying and tears to the One able to save Him from death, and He was heard because of His piety. Although He was a Son, He learned obedience from the things which He suffered. And having been made perfect, He became to all those who obey Him the source of eternal salvation" (Heb. 5:7–9).

Even God's Son was subject to the Father's training. He was born in the flesh like any other little boy, and He grew up to be a young man. Though He was God's Son, He still had to learn what it meant to obey His earthly parents. He was God in the flesh, but He also was man. From the beginning, Mary and Joseph taught Him obedience. The older He became, the more He learned. When Joseph died, Jesus took over the family business and became a carpenter. He was obedient. He did not say, "I'm the Son of God, and I can't be confined to a workshop. I have other things I need to do." Instead, He was committed to doing whatever the Father wanted Him to do. Because there was a human side to His life, He had to learn not only who He was but also who the Father wanted Him to be. He was the Messiah, the Savior, and God, but He also had to deal with the fact that His life contained a degree of humanity for a purpose. He was perfect in every way, but He had to learn obedience.

God Allows Us to Suffer to Teach Us to Trust Him

Peter declared, "The proof of your faith, being more precious than gold which is perishable, even though tested by fire, may be found to result in praise and glory and honor at the revelation of Jesus Christ" (1 Peter 1:7). Would you rather have an awesome, unwavering faith in God or the riches of this world? Even Christians have lost their focus when it comes to answering this question. They rationalize that they have to live and that God has promised to give good things to His children. So, they rush after the things of this world—things that they mistakenly perceive will bring happiness, fulfillment, and recognition. But when they obtain a degree of what the world prizes, they find that nothing in their collection of things and remembrances brings lasting joy and peace. They are restless, but they don't understand why. The happiest people in the world are those who have learned to trust and obey the Lord. When we do that, our anxiety level drops. The war that has been raging inside is over, and there is peace— peace between God and us.

He makes no apologies for sending suffering—whether it is physical, mental, or emotional. The author of Hebrews pointed out that "all discipline for the moment seems not to be joyful, but sorrowful; yet to those who have been trained by it, afterwards it yields the peaceful fruit of righteousness" (12:11). God allows adversity for the simple reason that He loves us too much to allow us to get by with being disobedient. He does not test our faith to discover our trust level. He knows that. He allows us to be tested to prove our faith. We are tested so that we can grow in our faith and be strengthened in our devotion to Him.

An example can be found in the area of tithing. If I were to ask you whether you believed in God, you probably would say yes. If I asked you whether you believed His Word was true, you would say yes again. If I took this a step further and asked whether you felt that you should give an offering to God, the answer would be yes a third time. However, if I asked, "Do you tithe the way God has commanded in His Word?" many would say no. And often the reason is a lack of faith in God's ability to provide for every need. You may say, "I know He can." But in another breath, you would have to admit, "I don't know if He will, so I hang on to as much as I can. But I do tithe some." From God's perspective, which is always the right one, it is all or nothing. Partial obedience is not obedience, and it certainly is no reflection of absolute trust in our omniscient God who has commanded us to trust and obey Him. Our lack of faith in an area like this one can position us for God's discipline. We may think that we will have more by holding back, but our lack of faith works against us.

First, we can never outgive God, so we are much better off doing what He has told us to do. Second, we miss His blessing when we don't follow His commandments. Something that appears to be relatively simple is really not insignificant. In fact, it is huge because it reveals the devotion of our hearts. Another thing we must consider is this: when God says that if we bring the tithe into the storehouse, He will bless us abundantly, He does not always mean that we will have a financial overflow. Anytime you and I are growing in our faith, we are getting richer on the inside. Yes, God will meet our financial needs, but we can achieve a richness with Him that is far greater than any amount of wealth we can find in this world.

Suffering Teaches Us to Depend upon His Grace and Goodness

In 2 Corinthians 12, Paul wrote, "I am well content with weaknesses, with insults, with distresses, with persecutions, with difficulties, for Christ's sake; for when I am weak, then I am strong" (v. 10). In Philippians, he restated this same thought:

> I rejoiced in the Lord greatly, that now at last you have revived your concern for me; indeed, you were concerned before, but you lacked opportunity. Not that I speak from want, for I have learned to be content in whatever circumstances I am. I know how to get along with humble means, and I also know how to live in prosperity; in any and every circumstance I have learned the secret of being filled and going hungry, both of having abundance and suffering need. I can do all things through Him who strengthens me. (4:10–13)

Paul had to rely on God for every single detail of his life. That was exactly what the Lord wanted him to do, and it is what He wants us to do too.

Most of us know the apostle suffered with "a thorn" in his flesh. We do not know what it was, but we are sure that it caused deep pain in his life. Paul had not disobeyed God, but the Lord certainly used this pain to draw him into an even closer relationship with Himself. When the apostle implored God to remove it, the Lord answered, "My grace is sufficient for you, for power is perfected in weakness" (2 Cor. 12:9). God's grace sustained him, and the same is true in your life. There may be something you long to experience. Or there could be "a thorn" in your flesh. It may be an illness or a person—someone who has caused great difficulty for you. You have prayed and asked God to remove it or to bring relief, but the problem remains and you are suffering. Why not change your focus and ask Him to allow you to see this experience from His perspective?

Paul did not want to suffer, but he became content when he realized that God had given this adversity for a reason. Then he had no problem saying, "Most gladly, therefore, I will rather boast about my weaknesses, so that the power of Christ may dwell in me. Therefore I am well content with weaknesses" (vv. 9–10). God teaches us tremendous lessons of faith in times of hardship. He refocuses our lives so that our hearts are trained on Him and not on our selfish desires. Knowing God and being known by Him should be your top priority. When it is, you will understand how He is working to train, mold, and shape you so you can understand His ways and live in the joy and hope He offers.

After a recent Sunday morning service, a woman came forward and told me that her brother had died in an automobile accident. She said, "Pastor, I can't even pray. The hurt is so deep. Please pray for me. I feel locked up inside and can't form the words to pray to God." We did exactly that: we prayed for her and asked God to wrap His arms of compassion around her. Some people who are suffering are completely perplexed. There is nothing in God's Word that tells us we will understand why He allows pain to touch our lives. But because we know He is faithful, we also can know that He works in times of suffering to draw us nearer to Himself. I have told the members of my congregation that as painful as adversity is, some of the greatest lessons of faith that I have learned have come as a result of the personal pain I have felt. Without a shadow of doubt, God uses adversity for our good and His glory.

Suffering Purifies Us

A person with a pure heart has pure motives. Many times when we think of purity, immorality comes to mind, and we reason that we're okay because we are not involved in it. But having purity of mind and heart also means we are not seeking to get our own way. Have you ever had someone pay you a compliment, and then a day or so later she comes back to you with a personal request? I'm not saying that every time someone says, "You look nice," her motives are impure. But there are times when people use compliments or other advantages to get what they want. Deep inside they know their motives are not pure. Therefore, they do something to gain your attention and motivate you to see a situation from their perspective. They are being deceptive, but they never would admit it. God sees straight through this behavior.

When Satan seeks to attack us, the first place he turns is the mind. Every day we are storing countless images and messages that can be retrieved in a fraction of a second. Because of the complexity of our brains, we cannot just decide what will be erased and what will be retained. Everything ends up being stored somewhere, and if we have a habit of viewing and listening to the things that God calls sinful, then we are going to have trouble not just for today but for a while. Therefore, Paul instructed us to be pure in heart and mind:

Be imitators of God, as beloved children; and walk in love, just as Christ also loved you and gave Himself up for us, an offering and a sacrifice to God as a fragrant aroma. But immorality or any impurity or greed must not even be named among you, as is proper among saints; and there must be no filthiness and silly talk, or coarse jesting, which are not fitting, but rather giving of thanks. For this you know with certainty, that no immoral or impure person or covetous man, who is an idolater, has an inheritance in the kingdom of Christ and God. Let no one deceive you with empty words, for because of these things the wrath of God comes upon the sons of disobedience. Therefore do not be partakers with them; for you were formerly darkness, but now you are Light in the Lord; walk as children of Light. (Eph. 5:1–8)

If sin or temptation is appealing to you, you have some work to do. If you are tempted by an action and tell yourself, *No one will know, and if someone does, it won't matter*, you are positioning yourself for a spiritual fall. Here is what happens: temptation comes, and most people try to rationalize their feelings. Sin begins with a thought. If this is not checked, it will grow into a feeling, and if we do not stand against it, we will end up giving in to it and acting on our feelings. When this continues, sin quickly becomes a habit, and a habit becomes a stronghold for the enemy to establish a base camp in our lives. A pure heart desires to be holy and righteous before God. There is no way to be dishonest and pure at the same time. This is because purity requires absolute honesty. Many people want to feel God's strength in their lives. He empowers us to do great things, but when sin is present, this is not the case. There is no power in our lives as believers if we are involved in impurity or if we refuse to confess our sin to God. Therefore, we need to set a goal for our lives to become holy because He is holy.

Suffering Teaches Us Gratitude

Adversity is a sharp reminder that we are not in control; God is. Either we can thank Him for the difficulty, knowing that He will bring something good out of it, or we can become bitter.

There have been times in my life when I said, "This is so hard, Lord. How can I ever be grateful for this? Will I ever be able to thank You for this pain?" Without fail, He always reminds me that no matter how difficult my circumstances seem, He is right beside me, and He is allowing this hurt for a reason. Therefore, I can be grateful. I probably won't enjoy what I am experiencing, but I can thank Him for allowing the suffering because I know He is at work.

Paul wrote, "In everything give thanks; for this is God's will for you in Christ Jesus" (1 Thess. 5:18). He did not say, "Be grateful when you receive only good things from God. Be hopeful and filled with joy when life goes your way." Of course, God wants us to be happy when He blesses us. That is easy. But He also wants us to learn how to thank Him for the difficult times because when we do, we demonstrate our faith in Him. This underscores the fact that our lives are hidden in Him and we are focused on His will and nothing else. It is God's will for us to be grateful. Paul did not say, "In everything feel very thankful." He instructed us to be surrendered and to be grateful for God's love and affection even when the trial is so severe that we wonder whether we can continue.

Suffering Teaches Us How to Persevere

Our world is full of people who want to give up. Their hopes and dreams have been dashed, and they want to quit. I think about those who accepted Christ as their Savior and falsely assumed that they would never face difficulty again. This is not reality. We will face challenges until God calls us home to be with Him. And if we want to succeed, we must not give up. A person who has perseverance stays the course. I read that Thomas Edison tried more than a thousand times to create a light bulb that would work. I'm sure when people asked him about his project, he probably thought, *No, but I can tell you a thousand different ways it doesn't work.* We need to realize that he never gave up. He kept trying until he succeeded.

Perseverance declares, "I'm not quitting. I'm not giving up, no matter what happens." I remember when I began work on one of my college degrees. I wanted to quit every week for the first six weeks. Before I went to bed at night, I prayed and tried to explain to God just how hard the classes were. But deep inside, I knew that He was saying, *You can't quit now. You have to keep going forward.* Perseverance builds character. It trains us to stay on course rather than give up. You may miss the promotion at work, but God has something better coming your way. Don't pull up stakes when something goes wrong. Be determined to wait for God to make His will known to you. If you give up, you will never know the level of potential within your life.

Suffering Enables Us to Share in the Sufferings of Jesus Christ

A false teaching asserts that if you are experiencing hardship, sickness, or misfortune, you are not trusting God. This misbelief teaches that wealth, health, happiness, and prosperity are indicators of a strong spiritual faith and God's blessing. This is not true. Part of God's plan for our lives is for us to learn how to face adversity with unwavering faith. Paul suffered, but he was not a spiritual failure. Did he have a strong, vibrant faith in God? Yes.

Some people may tell you, "If you have enough faith, God will heal everything." We know from reading the Gospels that He can cure any illness. But He may not choose to do this. In fact, do you realize what you would miss if you were healthy all the time or if you never faced a serious challenge or failure? You would never learn how to identify with Jesus Christ's death on the cross. And any sickness or tragedy we experience pales when compared to what the Savior suffered. Nevertheless, we can identify to a lesser degree with His death and crucifixion, but we must come to a point where we have a desire to be like Him. In times of extreme pain the Cross becomes a source of tremendous power and hope. Paul wrote, "The word of the cross is foolishness to those who are perishing, but to us who are being saved it is the power of God" (1 Cor. 1:18).

Suffering Broadens Our Ministry

Paul mentioned on several occasions that he wanted to preach the gospel in Rome. As we read through the book of Acts, we can almost anticipate his arrival. But none of us would have chosen to place him there as a prisoner, and yet God did. He was imprisoned for his faith in Christ, but his confinement did not prevent God from accomplishing His will through the apostle. In Philippians, Paul wrote, "I want you to know, brethren, that my circumstances have turned out for the greater progress of the gospel, so that my imprisonment in the cause of Christ has become well known throughout the whole praetorian guard and to everyone else, and that most of the brethren, trusting in the Lord because of my imprisonment, have far more courage to speak the word of God without fear" (1:12–14). Paul knew without a shadow of doubt that the Lord placed him right in the middle of trouble, and he flourished.

God Restores Hope

When adversity strikes, do you feel panic or trust God? Don't overlook the fact that He is a restorer of hope: "The LORD blessed the latter days of Job more than his beginning" (Job 42:12). God gave the apostle Paul an entirely different ministry in Rome. As a result of his ministry in prison, the gospel spread throughout Rome. New Testament churches were strengthened and encouraged, and Paul had the opportunity to preach to people who never would have heard about the unconditional love and forgiveness of Jesus Christ. We should never seek to put God in a box. Paul knew something about the ways of God. He was walking in step with His will, and his ministry was broadened in ways that he never dreamed possible. God sees what we will never be able to see. He infinitely knows what will happen in the future. Suffering prepares you by training you to trust God and know that He is always at work in your life.

Chapter Nine

FORGIVEN!

Sometimes when I preach on the subject of salvation, I look out at my congregation, and I can sense that a subtle thought of deception runs through the minds of many people. It goes something like this: *Everyone knows how to be forgiven of sin.* The very idea of this jars me to respond with, *No, they don't.* Especially with an established congregation like we have at First Baptist Atlanta, it is extremely important to be aware that new people join our fellowship every Sunday. And there are plenty of others who have lingered along the sidelines of life for years, never making a commitment to Jesus Christ. To think that most of the people who attend our church are saved would be a deadly assumption.

Another point that we need to keep in mind is there are a lot of misconceptions about forgiveness of sin. Therefore, I'm going to distinguish between the forgiveness that leads to salvation and the forgiveness that is available for our daily sins. Before I do that, though, I want to tell you about a man I met years ago and immediately liked. He was a sharp businessman with a buoyant personality. And because he was such a savvy communicator, he quickly learned to talk and to act like a very committed believer. I would have been fooled, too, but something deep within me told me to be careful and not to take this man into my circle of friends.

Picking Up on Crucial Warning Signs

Over time, we saw each other at many functions, but the uneasiness that I felt in my spirit never let up. Later, when I was with this man in a more personal setting, I discovered what I felt deep inside, and it was the fact that he was not a believer. There was no evidence of a personal relationship with Jesus Christ, and there was almost an outward proclamation that he had managed to deceive many within the Christian community. I don't know that I would go so far as to say that this man wanted nothing to do with the Lord, but I would say that he was lost and his trickery and cunning, deceptive ways were very obvious.

The greatest hurt he inflicted was not on other people but on himself. Spiritually he was lost, and as abrupt and stark as this may sound, it is true: if God had chosen to end his life, he would have died and gone to hell. We are not saved by what we have. The right friends, a lot of money, power, position, fame, and anything else mean nothing to God. There is only one way to heaven—through faith in the Lord Jesus Christ. A person can store up wealth until he or she amasses a fortune, but not a single penny will bring the joy, peace, and happiness that God gives to those who accept His Son as their Savior.

We need to recognize how little we are involved in the process of salvation. God is the One who saves us by His grace. In Ephesians, Paul wrote,

Blessed be the God and Father of our Lord Jesus Christ, who has blessed us with every spiritual blessing in the heavenly places in Christ, just as *He chose us* in Him before the foundation of the world, that we would be holy and blameless before Him. In love *He predestined us to adoption* as sons through

Jesus Christ to Himself, according to the kind intention of His will, to the praise of the glory of His grace, which He freely bestowed on us in the Beloved. In Him we have redemption through His blood, the forgiveness of our trespasses, according to the riches of His grace which He lavished on us. (1:3–8, *emphasis added*)

Salvation was God's idea. He chose us. We did not choose Him. Throughout history, God has been working to bring mankind back into a right relationship with Him. Immediately following the Fall in the Garden of Eden, we see God's motivation at work. He goes to Adam and Eve, confronts them, disciplines them, and then covers them with skins from animals that He killed. It grieved the heart of God to see His creation fall. But even this act of rebellion and sin could not prevent the love and purpose of God from continuing. This was the first blood to be shed as the result of man's sin. However, it was also the one event that released the pendulum and began the countdown to the Savior's birth, death, and resurrection. The word *redemption* means release or freedom as a result of payment. You and I are redeemed or bought back by Christ's atoning death on Calvary's cross.

How Does God Save You?

Forgiveness, as it relates to salvation, is the work of God. He delivers us from the penalty of sin, which is eternal death. Salvation is His gracious gift to you and me, as Paul noted, "By grace you have been saved through faith; and that not of yourselves, it is the gift of God; not as a result of works, so that no one may boast" (Eph. 2:8–9). The apostle continued by making it very clear that we have been saved for a purpose, and that is to glorify God: "For we are His workmanship, created in Christ Jesus for good works, which God prepared beforehand so that we would walk in them" (v. 10). Once they are saved, lots of believers go to work thinking that they can prove their love to God through their service. But there is only one way to demonstrate our devotion to Him, and that is through total surrender. We offer our lives to Him, knowing that His gift of eternal life outweighs anything we could do or hope to accomplish in His name. A simple, heartfelt confession of unbridled love for Him ignites a firestorm of glory and praise in heaven.

God does not change, and He does not save us on the basis of who we are, what we have done, or what we will do in the future. He saves us because He loves us and because of the work that His Son did for us on the cross. It is a universal fact that each one of us has sinned against God. Like Adam and Eve, we have been found guilty of our trespasses and, rightfully under the law of God, deserve death. We have fallen short of what is required of us and of what is necessary to be acceptable in His sight (Rom. 3:23). But He has chosen to provide a way by which our sins—past, present, and future—can be forgiven for eternity.

God's promise is to deliver us from the penalty of sin and then to give us the opportunity to come to know Him personally through an intimate relationship. Many people who are separated from God do not even realize that they are in a very volatile position. They tell themselves, *I'm not so sinful; I'm not as bad as other people.* They compare themselves to others and many times to believers who are not living dedicated lives instead of comparing themselves to Jesus Christ, the holy Son of God. They have a sin problem, and yet they try to find a way to lessen its effects. There is no way to do this.

Either you have surrendered your life to Christ, or you have refused. It is just that plain and just that simple. Every once in a while I will hear someone say, "Oh, I'm going to do that [accept Jesus as my Savior] one day but not now." Or he may say, "I'm going to wait until I'm good and ready," to which I reply, "There may not be a 'good and ready time.'" God can take your life tonight, and then you will have no more opportunities—no more chances and no more afterthoughts.

I remember years ago talking to a member of our church about her brother. She did not know whether he was a Christian, and then suddenly he was killed in an accident. We talked on several occasions about how she could come to grips with the reality of his death. Because of the impact it had on her and her parents, who were believers, she had to come to a point of acceptance. Her brother had the same opportunity she had been given, and yet he had said no. Some people talk about what they will say when they stand in God's presence. Some tell how they will explain to the Lord why they have been so rebellious. But I totally believe that when we are in God's presence, we will all be speechless. The only words we will utter will be words of praise and adoration. And I don't think we will have the ability to stand in defiance before Him. Some may shake their fists at Him in anger, but in heaven's holy light, the most we will do is bow in reverence and honor to Him—the Lord of lords and the King of kings. In talking about His return, Jesus said, "Be on the alert then, for you do not know the day nor the hour" (Matt. 25:13). And He told His disciples that only God knows the hour and the moment of His return:

> Be dressed in readiness, and keep your lamps lit. Be like men who are wait-
> ing for their master when he returns from the wedding feast, so that they
> may immediately open the door to him when he comes and knocks. Blessed
> are those slaves whom the master will find on the alert when he comes. . . .
> But be sure of this, that if the head of the house had known at what hour
> the thief was coming, he would not have allowed his house to be broken
> into. You too, be ready; for the Son of Man is coming at an hour that you
> do not expect. (Luke 12:35–37, 39–40)

While these verses are based on Christ's return, they also demonstrate the immediacy of God's command to be ready at any point for His call. Salvation comes as a response to His work in a person's life. But it is not something that we decide will happen on a certain day and at a certain time. The hour of decision belongs to God and God alone. The Holy Spirit prepares our hearts, pricks our conscience with conviction that feels like guilt, and exposes our sin and shame. In the midst of these is also a sense of God's divine love drawing us—wooing us—to His Son. Jesus Christ came into this world to die for our sins. Even before He drew His first breath, the shadow of the cross was draped over His life. Therefore, it is not just enough to believe that Jesus is. We must know that He is the Son of God, the only way to salvation, and our living Lord.

Many people believe that Jesus lived, but they do not believe in Him as the divine Son of God, who is sinless and the only One who can take away our sins. The only reason God forgives sin is that His Son paid our sin debt in full on the cross. Think back to what God did for Adam and Eve after they had sinned and were banished from God's presence. He made coverings of animal skins for them. By its very nature, sin demands payment for the wrong that was done. On our own we have nothing to offer God. There is nothing within us that is good enough, great enough, or powerful enough to save us. We need Someone to make a sacrificial offering for us so that we can be forgiven. The only Person who can do this is the sinless, blameless, spotless Lamb of God—Jesus Christ.

When you accept Him as your Savior, your life is covered by His blood. You are sealed with an unbreakable seal that proclaims your forgiveness and innocence before God and all of Satan's forces. Before you accepted Him as your Savior, a gulf separated you from Him. But when you drew near, bowed at the foot of His cross, professed your sin and your need of forgiveness, you were brought near to Him. This is when He saved you—not just for a little while but for eternity. The chains of sin, shame, and unmentionable guilt fell away, and you were freed from your bondage.

Salvation is a decision that you must make. It is personal and not something that your father or mother can decide for you. Being baptized as a child does not make you a Christian. You may be a church member, but you may not know Jesus Christ. In fact, everyone in your family may go to church every Sunday and own a Bible, but not be saved. Salvation is a personal decision between you and God. Many people, however, have been misled and falsely assume church membership or baptism is all they need to be saved. There is no truth in this assumption.

You may be a good person, but this does not mean you will go to heaven. Jesus admonished His followers with these words:

> Truly, truly, I say to you, you seek Me, not because you saw signs, but because you ate of the loaves and were filled. Do not work for the food which perishes, but for the food which endures to eternal life, which the Son of Man will give to you, for on Him the Father, God, has set His seal. . . . I am the bread of life; he who comes to Me will not hunger, and he who believes in Me will never thirst. But I said to you that you have seen Me, and yet do not believe. All that the Father gives Me will come to Me, and the one who comes to Me I will certainly not cast out. For I have come down from heaven, not to do My own will, but the will of Him who sent Me. This is the will of Him who sent Me, that of all that He has given Me I lose nothing, but raise it up on the last day. For this is the will of My Father, that everyone who beholds the Son and believes in Him will have eternal life, and I Myself will raise him up on the last day. (John 6:26–27, 35–40)

There is only one way to know God, and that is through His Son, through His Holy Spirit, and through His written Word. Jesus did not stop with this explanation. Four verses later, He summed up everything: "No one can come to Me unless the Father who sent Me draws him; and I will raise him up on the last day" (v. 44). The Holy Spirit is the One who convicts you of sin, brings you to the realization that you need God, and then convicts you that you have ignored Him and chosen to turn your back to

Him. Until the work of the Spirit transpires in your life, you will not be saved. Your human nature does not want to draw near to God. Mankind just doesn't naturally want to get right with Him. Something has to happen because the natural man cannot receive the things that are of God. There is no spiritual discernment and no desire to live for Him.

In Romans, Paul reminded us, "There is none righteous, not even one; there is none who understands, there is none who seeks for God; all have turned aside" (3:10–12). When His Spirit begins to work in your life, suddenly you sense a hunger, a desire for Him that you cannot explain. Trials come and you cry out and wonder whether He cares, but you also have a fresh sense of knowing that He does. You are saved and you are His. In Romans 8, Paul explained,

> We know that God causes all things to work together for good to those who love God, to those who are called according to His purpose. For those whom He foreknew, He also predestined to become conformed to the image of His Son, so that He would be the firstborn among many brethren; and these whom He predestined, He also called; and these whom He called, He also justified; and these whom He justified, He also glorified. What then shall we say to these things? If God is for us, who is against us? (vv. 28–31)

God is the One who calls to us. Moses did not address the burning bush. God called to him. Abraham did not say, "I will go this way because I think this is what is best." He sensed God's leading, and he answered the call in obedience. The Spirit of God was at work in these men's hearts, just as He is working in ours today. He woos the lost man, convicts him of sin, and then makes an awesome offer of eternal salvation.

Before we are saved, we must accept four truths and act on them:

1. *We must realize that without Jesus Christ, there is no eternal life.* It does not matter how much material wealth we have. If we do not have a personal

relationship with the Savior, we will spend an eternity in hell separated from God and His goodness.

2. *We must have some knowledge or understanding of who Jesus Christ is.* When people say, "I have always believed in Jesus," I ask them to tell me when they came to a point of saving knowledge of who He is. I also ask if they have ever confessed their sins to Him, acknowledging their sinfulness that has alienated them from God. And are they aware that if they continue to refuse God's merciful love and grace demonstrated on the cross, they will die and go to hell? These questions may sound harsh, but the harsher truth is that if we fail to tell others about God's forgiveness and salvation, they will die separated from Him and will spend an eternity in absolute anguish of soul and spirit. There is only one way to have eternal life, and it begins at the foot of the cross as we profess our faith in the Son of God.

3. *We must demonstrate faith in Christ.* No man or woman can save us. Knowing a godly grandparent or parent does nothing for us in this area. Either we come to know Him on our own, or we remain alienated from Him by our pride and sin. Paul wrote, "If you confess with your mouth Jesus as Lord, and *believe* in your heart that God raised Him from the dead, you will be saved" (Rom. 10:9, *emphasis added*). Whenever you see the word *believe* in the New Testament, you automatically know that it is a word of action. It leads somewhere, and in this case it is a doorway to salvation through faith in Christ. Therefore, when a person says that he truly believes in God's Son, he is saying that he believes in the Lord Jesus Christ from a scriptural point of view; he is willing to acknowledge the lordship of Christ. Not only that, but the person admits that he is a sinner and needs a Savior. Action takes place because biblical faith and repentance cannot be separated. In other words, if you truly believe that you are a sinner saved by grace, you will ask God to forgive your sins and make a commitment to turn away from the very things that bring shame and sorrow to your life.

I have listened to moms and dads talk about their children and how they have drifted in their faith or their unwillingness to accept Christ. Parents need to teach godly principles to their sons and daughters. They need to pray with them and counsel them with godly morals and values. But there may come a time when that child makes a decision to turn away from the truth that he has heard at home and in church. When this happens, parents should stand firm in their faith, but also pray that God would be the One who makes His will clear to that young person.

We can beg and plead, but still there may not be a lasting change. Through the power of His Spirit, God is the only One who can sufficiently convict someone of sin. He uses parents, but there are times when He is the only One who can speak and be heard. If this is the case, we need to trust Him and allow Him to work in the lives of loved ones. As difficult as it is, some lessons can be learned only through adversity.

4. *We must repent from sin.* Jesus opened the minds of His disciples "to understand the Scriptures, and He said to them, 'Thus it is written, that the Christ would suffer and rise again from the dead the third day, and that repentance for forgiveness of sins would be proclaimed in His name to all the nations, beginning from Jerusalem. You are witnesses of these things'" (Luke 24:45–48). In order to understand the ways of God and to walk in step with Him, your mind must be renewed through salvation and through the reading of His Word. Jesus opened their minds. He spoke His truth to them. There is no escaping this. We take a step toward learning and understanding His will and ways when we acknowledge our need of Him. Salvation begins with our dropping our pride, confessing our need and sin, and then lifting our hearts up to Him in true repentance. Jesus stated, "Unless you repent, you will all likewise perish" (Luke 13:3).

Forgiven, Saved, and Tempted

I looked across my desk into the face of a young man who had been a Christian only a few months. He was always down front, taking notes, every

Sunday morning and Wednesday evening. Despite his recent church attendance, he had yielded to temptation and become entangled in sin. After he told me his story, we sat for a moment in silence, just letting the weight of what had happened sink in. While I felt badly for him, I also realized that it always is stunning for someone to experience the consequences of sin. But unless we are forced to do this, we will usually repeat the offense. There is a difference between the forgiveness that leads to salvation and the forgiveness that we, as believers, receive. The moment this young man confessed his sin to God and asked for forgiveness, God did just that. He forgave him, but the consequences of his decision could not be reversed.

Christ's forgiveness for my salvation took care of the penalty of my sin. One way that God works in my life is to set me free from an eternal punishment. Jesus paid my sin debt in full. Every sin that I have committed or will commit is forgiven. But I still need to acknowledge the wrong choices and decisions I have made as a believer. I'm forgiven from the aspect of my eternal destiny, but I still need to receive God's forgiveness whenever I yield to temptation.

When I explain this truth, I often use an analogy. Think for a moment about being dressed in white. This is exactly how God views your life the moment you turn your life over to Him. But then you receive an invitation to go down into a coal mine. Immediately you think about how much fun it would be to see the inside of the mine, but you also realize that you are not dressed for such an adventure. You think about declining, yet curiosity and pressure from your friends lead you to accept the offer. The next thing you know you are in the tunnel, and you are being covered with dust and grime. You did not listen to the warning signals that were going off inside you. And you ignored what you knew was right, and now you need to be cleansed.

We live in a corrupt, sinful, wicked, vile world. Profanity, lewdness, and all kinds of dirt and filth are within our reach. People become angry, resentful, or hostile, and before you know it, they have lashed out at you and you react by mirroring their actions. You come home in the evenings, and you notice that your children have not done what you told them to do. Their rooms are a mess, they are chatting on the phone or text messaging friends, and you lose your temper. Guess what? When you respond to a situation with anger, you have just reached out and touched the dusty, black grime of a coal mine and wiped it on your white overcoat. But you can ask for forgiveness and become completely clean again. You never lose your salvation. Your life is sealed with an eternal stamp signifying that you belong to Jesus Christ. Even so, you can become spiritually dirty and in need of God's cleansing touch.

Our need for a Savior does not end the moment we are saved. We need Jesus at every turn in life. We need His protection, provision, guidance, and forgiveness. We need to come to a point where we realize that His power within us is greater than any temptation to yield to sin. But when we do fall, and each one of us will at some point, we have an Advocate—Someone who will stand with us before God.

John gave us this hopeful look into the ways of God: "My little children, I am writing these things to you so that you may not sin. And if anyone sins, we have an Advocate with the Father, Jesus Christ the righteous; and He Himself is the propitiation for our sins; and not for ours only, but also for those of the whole world. By this we know that we have come to know Him, if we keep His commandments" (1 John 2:1–3). John did not say we would never sin. He said, "And if anyone sins."

God knows the power of temptation, but His goal for us is to resist the enemy by saying no to sin (James 4:7). When we do, we find that we have Someone standing not only with us but between us and Satan—our accuser. Moses, Abraham, David, Joshua, Mary of Bethany, and many more drew so close to God that they understood that engaging in sin would create a spiritual gulf between them and the Lord. We cannot engage in sin and remain in close fellowship with Him. Paul admonished us not to become too intimately involved with nonbelievers: "Do not be bound together with unbelievers; for what partnership have righteousness and lawlessness, or what fellowship has light with darkness?" (2 Cor. 6:14). The apostle was writing to express his concern over the Corinthians' involvement with false teachers who did not believe that Jesus was God's Son and Messiah. His words also are stern warnings to us about the depth of our personal relationship with people who are godless and have no desire to know the Savior.

On several occasions, I have had the opportunity to warn believers not to enter into a marriage commitment with an unsaved person. They falsely believe that they can "help" their future marriage partner come to know the Lord, and even though this very thing may take place, there is a price for disobedience. God instructed the nation of Israel to remain pure and free from idolatry and not to worship the gods of their enemies. They did not listen. They intermarried, and soon their devotion to God began to wane. They brought idols into their homes and worshiped them. As a result of their actions, God disciplined them, allowing their enemies to overthrow them and take them into captivity.

I have also listened as Christian businessmen acknowledged their huge error by believing that they could own and run a company with a nonbeliever. Some made a lot of money, and they were successful. But most agree that the stress and pressure from being connected on a personal level with someone who does not know Jesus Christ is tremendous and very exhausting. God will protect and provide for you if you are working alongside nonbelievers at your job. Most people are in secular businesses. The problem comes when we become joined with another person who does not share our spiritual values. The mind-set and moral values are not the same.

Before a person is saved, he is separated from the Lord. He is alienated from God, and the Bible tells us that he is walking in spiritual darkness and not the light of God's truth. He is living under the wrath of God; he is living according to the ways of the world and not the ways of God. He is empty-minded because the mind of the natural man cannot discern spiritual truth. He is motivated by the lust of the flesh and is dead in his trespasses and sin. Think about this: How can a person understand the mind of God or talk with Him in prayer if he has chosen to deny God and live a separate life? He can't.

The moment we say no to drawing near to God, we limit what we can know and understand about Him. This is completely true of the lost man or woman, but it can also be true to a certain degree of the person who is saved but is not living a Christian lifestyle. Too many believers have walked away from God. He has not moved, but they have. They may be saved, yet when adversity comes, they cry out, not understanding one single thing about His work in their lives. On more than one occasion, I have sat in my church office and listened to a believer talk about how she can no longer trust God. She may have made a series of wrong choices, but she believes God could have prevented all the negative things from happening. It is true that He can, but as I have said throughout this book, His desire is to draw us into an intimate relationship with Him. Sin has consequences, and God will not change the principles He has established. Therefore, when we choose to disobey Him, we suffer. If we want to know why something has happened, we need to move closer to Him not further away. We also need to seek His forgiveness when we sin.

You cannot mix sin and purity, so you must decide which one you will choose. Be careful in your choice because one leads to inexpressible joy, peace, and security, while the other leads to isolation, insecurity, regret, and deep sorrow. We cannot fully understand the work of the Holy Spirit until we accept Jesus Christ as our Savior and then surrender all that we are to Him. Once we surrender ourselves to Him, our lives change. We may have moments when we drift in our devotion, but there is an irresistible sense of love for God within our hearts that we are not willing to compromise. We can know the truth about sin and its path to destruction, but we must be

God-focused and not self-centered or worldly minded. There is no way to combine either of these with the truth of God and have a situation that works and is pleasing to the Lord. He demands our full devotion. Anything less has serious consequences.

When His disciples wanted to know how to pray effectively, Jesus taught them a prayer. I want you to consider praying this prayer each day or at least as often as God leads you:

> Our Father who is in heaven,
> Hallowed be Your name.
> Your kingdom come
> Your will be done,
> On earth as it is in heaven.
> Give us this day our daily bread.
> And forgive us our debts, as we also have forgiven our debtors.
> And do not lead us into temptation, but deliver us from evil.
> For Yours is the kingdom and the power and the glory forever. Amen.
>   (Matt. 6:9–13)

The Savior wanted to teach His followers *how to maintain the right focus.* They noticed His relationship with the heavenly Father was tremendously close, and they wanted to experience the same thing. They watched Him go off by Himself to pray and be alone with God. Whenever there was a need or a problem, Jesus had the answer. We know that He is God in the flesh, but we also know that He has an incredible relationship with the Father. He desired more than anything to be with Him. And remember on the cross that while the pain was excruciating, the greater pain came as a result of bearing our sins and knowing that God the Father could not look on Him. He was separated from the One whom He loved more than anything else. You cannot separate God from His Son or from His Spirit. They are one, and yet for a brief moment in time, this very thing took place between the Father and Jesus while He was clothed with our unrighteousness. But the power of God shattered sin's grasp, and we have been given the power to live a life of extreme joy and freedom from sin—all because Jesus died for our sins.

He instructed His disciples to begin each day by acknowledging who God is: their heavenly Father, the awesome God of the universe, sovereign in power, and over all things. There is something tremendously faith building in saying the various names of Jesus—Prince of Peace (Isa. 9:6), Almighty God (Rev. 4:8), the Light of the World (John 8:12), Faithful and True (Rev. 19:11), Wonderful Counselor (Isa. 9:6). In many cases, they define His power, who He is, and what He will do for us. He doesn't just forgive our sin; He restores the hope that we have lost and the purity that sin tried to strip away. He also taught His followers how to acknowledge their sin. They knew Him, but just knowing Christ is not enough in this case.

We must acknowledge and agree with God that what we have done is wrong. His Son's death on the cross was sufficient payment for our sins, but we must take action. We must say, "Lord, what I did was wrong. Please forgive me." At this point, God applies His forgiveness to our lives. Until you experience this level of forgiveness, you cannot live to your greatest potential.

If you, as a believer, are carrying around sin in your life, you are going to be weighed down. You can't enjoy life fully, and you certainly cannot experience God's blessings and goodness. A sin such as jealousy will steal your joy. Envy, resentment, bitterness, and anger will prevent you from being all you can be through Christ. Your attention is not focused when you are thinking about something that is wrong in God's eyes. Greed limits your ability to know what God is calling you to do. An endless pursuit of worldly fame and wealth will harden your heart to the simple pleasures that He gives each day. Lust, greed, and immorality deaden your heart and spirit to such a degree that you cannot hear the voice of God. You become spiritually deaf to the principles written in His Word. And over time, you will find that you are making one mistake after another.

Jesus comes to a crucial part in the prayer when He commands them to forgive those who have hurt them. It is one thing to ask God to forgive us, especially when we are hurting and know we are out of step with Him. But it is an entirely different issue to forgive others when we believe they have wronged us in some way. Yet this is what He commands us to do. We cannot ignore God's principles. If we want to know and understand the depths of His love, we must obey Him.

Over the years when I've talked with people who were struggling, the subject always came around to forgiveness. Did they know that God forgave them, and were they willing to forgive those who hurt them? Many times they told me, "I can't forgive this person. You don't know what he did to me." It is true that I don't, but here is what I do know: unforgiveness is like a poison leaking into your system. It has a devastating effect on the body and the emotions. Friends who are doctors and psychologists have confirmed this and have said that much of the stress that people deal with each day often comes from hidden anger, frustration, disappointment, and a lack of forgiveness. When you forgive someone, you are not saying that what he or she did was right or even okay. You are saying that you want to be free from the memory and the bondage associated with the past. You want to do what Jesus commanded, and that is to forgive so that you can be forgiven for all the many sins you have committed or will commit in the future.

Unforgiveness affects my prayer life. If there is unforgiveness in my heart, I won't be focused or sure that God will answer me. It is more than a distraction; it is a stumbling block, and it is the reason God instructs us to obey Him in this area. While He was dying on Calvary's cross, Jesus prayed, "Father, forgive them; for they do not know what they are doing" (Luke 23:34). When we practice this principle, God pours out His blessings on us. We don't even have to ask Him to bless us; we sense an incredible joy rise up within us. And we also gain a sense of peace that is unshakable. In His way and in His timing God will deal with those who have hurt us. Our responsibility is to forgive and let go of anything and everything that would prevent us from knowing God and walking in fellowship with Him each day.

Living the Christian life is serious, and forgiveness is a foundational part of it. You cannot substitute good works for sin and receive the gift of salvation. Neither can you refuse to forgive others and think you can erase your bitterness by doing acts of kindness. If you fail to forgive those who have wronged you, you will end up hurting in a far greater way. I'm sure that someone who is reading these words has been hurt greatly. I can identify with that hurt. One of the more difficult moments in my life brought tremendous hurt, and I had to make a conscious choice to forgive. I knew from the beginning that no matter what happened, I had to maintain a forgiving spirit.

You may think you can't, and you are probably right. The only way you can completely forgive wrongs done to you is through trusting Jesus Christ and remembering that He forgave you. He never has asked and never will ask you to make a single payment toward your salvation or the forgiveness of your daily sins. He paid that debt for you in full. You have been declared not guilty. He has justified you and sealed you with an unbreakable, eternal seal of love, power, and goodness. You can lie down tonight and go to sleep because He is with you and He is your salvation.

Is there anyone you need to forgive? If there is, my prayer is that you would not wait another minute to extend the same forgiveness that you have been given. In some cases, it may be impossible and not practical for you to contact that individual. God will show you what is best. But the most important thing you can do is to pray and turn that person over to God along with all your unforgiveness.

Chapter Ten

THE GOD
OF ABSOLUTE LOVE

At the end of a Sunday morning sermon, a young man came forward to speak with me. I immediately knew he was eager to tell me something about his life. He had driven a long way to express his gratitude for our In Touch radio program. He told me that several years earlier he had been in prison for a serious crime. Up to that point, he had never heard about the love of God. Over the course of several weeks, he kept noticing a certain group of inmates were allowed to listen to a program on the radio. Boredom and the desire to be with others were the catalysts that God used to get him to join the group. He explained how God began to work in his life. He said, "I think I finally came to the end—or what I believed was the end—of all hope. I wondered why I was here and if it was worth continuing. I listened to you but thought, *This stuff can't be true.* But I kept listening. Then one day I remember you saying: 'God loves you just the way you are. He doesn't love the sin you are involved with, but He loves you.' My family members had turned their backs on me, and my friends were just plain tired of me promising to get my life straightened out but never following through by doing it. My first thought was, *I bet I have worn God out too. He couldn't possibly love me. I'm too far gone.* But I discovered the opposite. He does love me!"

As I listened to this man tell what God had done for him, I remember thinking how hard it must have been for him to consider his life as being over—or at a point where he did not believe it was worth living or drawing another breath. I also know there are people who will read these words and say that they can relate to this man's story. They don't understand how God can possibly love them or want to have anything to do with them. Many find it hard to believe that He does. For years, they have bought in to the enemy's lie that tells them that they have gone too far, and the Lord is going to let them go and never save them. It's just not true.

This young man was one of them. He believed that he was never going to amount to anything. So he might as well continue living like the devil. But God got a hold of his life. He told me how the Lord spoke to him through one of the messages he heard, and suddenly he began to entertain the thought that there could be hope. Then one night in the darkness of his jail cell, he surrendered his life to Christ and went to sleep for the first time as a free man. He became a regular listener of our broadcast. He also began reading and studying his Bible. Before he knew it, he started praying and quoting back to God the promises he was learning: "Lord, You have told me that You love me, and I believe that You do. Show me how I can live each day for You, even in this place of confinement." God did exactly that—He began to teach the young man principles of truth, which became foundational building blocks in his life. They taught him to think differently about God and about himself.

One of the most important lessons he learned was that while he was a sinner, he also was forgiven, and he was saved by the wondrous grace of God. He knew that his life contained nothing of value to match God's priceless gift. But he realized that was the way it was supposed to be— none of him and all of God. He had been given a second chance at life because God loved him, and he could hardly contain his joy. Months that were supposed to be spent in dread and sorrow became avenues of joy, peace, and hope. His family might have acted as if he was forgotten, but he was right in the crosshairs of God's radar. The Lord knew all about him and loved him. "God transformed my life," he said. "Today, I am a successful businessman who can't wait to tell others about what He has done for me. It was the love of God that grabbed my heart and life. Knowing that He did not give up on me changed me. Before I met Jesus, I was very hard-hearted, but that all changed." He smiled and said, "I guess you can say that love did change me. I never thought someone would care, but then I met Him and I know He does."

Love changes us. It changes the way we view life, the way we respond to others, and the way we view our circumstances. If we feel unloved, abandoned, forsaken, and rejected, we act accordingly. Even though it is not true, we will begin to think that it is, and we will reflect this self-image to people around us. Not only this, but like the man in the story above, we will wonder how anyone, especially God, could love us.

The Lord has many attributes. For example, He is a God of love, justice, mercy, holiness, and righteousness. He is omnipotent, which means He is all-powerful. He is omniscient—He knows all things. He sees the past, the present, and the future. We may remember a personal mistake we made in the past, but God chooses not to recall it. He knows it is there, but once we ask Him to forgive us, He will never bring it up again. He may allow us to recall it from time to time, especially if we are tempted by sin, but He is not going to condemn us because that is not His nature. Love, forgiveness, and restoration are at the heart of who He is. He also is omnipresent, which means He is with you right now. He is present with every believer in the world. He knows what is taking place in the Middle East and at the same time is aware of what is going on in your life. Nothing escapes His knowledge. He is God, and He is over all things. He lives within us through the power of His

Holy Spirit, who is not confined by time, distance, or circumstances. He is eternal—the beginning and the end—the Alpha and the Omega.

The God who declares His love for you and me is the One who loved David, Peter, Joshua, and everyone who has ever lived. He is the same. Nothing about Him has changed because His attributes are infinite and immutable. He is absolutely perfect. His single greatest desire is that you and I would have a deep, intimate relationship with Him. It is not enough for God to declare His love. He wants us to know Him and enjoy the peace and security that come from being in His care.

Some people may think that He sees what they have done in the past and that somehow His love for them has changed. It hasn't. Or perhaps someone reading these words has drifted away from Him. You once were very close to the Savior, but sin has changed the way you feel about Him. Remember, Adam hid from God. He ran away out of fear because he believed Satan's lie. I want you to know that God has not moved. Even though you have said yes to sin many times, He still loves you. He doesn't agree with what you are doing, but He has chosen to love you. Period. This is the end of the discussion from the perspective of His eternal love. Regardless of what has happened, God sees only possibilities and absolute potential in your life. He doesn't operate in some capsule of time. He knows the beginning of your life, and He also knows where He wants you to end. He always has the future in mind. He knows what He wants to do and intends to do, and how He will accomplish it in your life. It is always much more than you think.

How do you reach your maximum potential? How do you avoid floating through life with the attitude of just getting by? You begin by understanding that His love for you is eternal and unconditional. You may wonder, *Don't I need to do something in order to achieve this?* The answer is no. There is only one way, and that is through a personal relationship with Jesus Christ—the Person whose love for you never changes. Once you tap into the truth that your Creator loves you, you will gain an entirely different perspective of why and how He loves you.

- His love is *perfect*.

- His love is *sacrificial*—He laid down the life of His Son so that you could be saved from your sins.

- His love is a *gift* that is immeasurable in nature—you cannot measure the love of God.

- His love is *incomprehensible*—you cannot explain it fully.

- His love is *unconditional*—you cannot lose it and you cannot work to gain more of it. The moment you accept Christ as your Savior, you gain all that God has for you. It also means that He loves you without restriction.

- His love is *unchanging*—God loves you at every stage in life regardless of what you have done.

- His love is *eternal*—nothing can stop God from loving you. I have heard people say, "When I get my life straightened out, then I'll be able to accept the fact that He cares for me." It will never happen because He wants you to know and accept His love right now.

If God loved us on the basis of anything other than what is within Him, we would never know true, unconditional love. If there were a way to earn His love, then the Christian life would be based on performance and not on what He did for us. But it is not. It is completely the result of His unconditional love for you and me. Nothing but His shed blood, as a sacrificial gift and offering, will work.

Those Whom Jesus Loved

To emphasize this point, we are going to explore the situations surrounding the lives of several people Jesus met during His life on earth and the ways in which His love changed them.

Jesus chose *Peter* to become one of His disciples, even though He knew the fisherman was brash and very outspoken. Peter was a successful business-man, so he was accustomed to directing people who worked for him. When we study his life, we quickly learn that Jesus had to keep a close watch on him. He realized that given enough room, Peter would begin to direct Him and the others. He was always stepping out in front of the group and speak-ing without sincerely thinking through what he was about to say.

On one occasion, Jesus had to strongly rebuke him with words that I know must have seemed abrupt, but they were necessary. Peter was impet-uous, and he wanted Jesus to do what he felt was best. A short time earlier, he confessed Jesus as the Messiah—something that only God could reveal to him (Matt. 16:15–17). Later after the Savior told His followers of His impending death and resurrection, Peter pulled Him aside and said, "God forbid it, Lord! This shall never happen to You" (v. 22). Jesus dealt imme-diately with Peter's self-centered evaluation. He said, "Get behind Me, Satan! You are a stumbling block to Me; for you are not setting your mind on God's interests, but man's" (v. 23). It is typical to think after you have made a huge mistake that God is disappointed, but He knew what you were going to do even before you did it. Jesus chose Peter to become a disciple not on the basis of what he would do correctly but on the basis of His eternal love. He understood all the ins and outs of Peter's personality, and He saw potential in the fisherman's life. He also knew that Peter was in training and was being molded for God's service.

When we hear his story, we often criticize Peter for his impetuous actions, but more than likely, a part of us wishes that we could have his level of faith. During a horrendous storm on the Sea of Galilee, Peter was the only disciple who got out of the boat and began walking on the water to Jesus. The others were paralyzed with fear—but not Peter. And even though he began to sink, his effort is noteworthy. His most vivid failure came after Christ's crucifixion when he denied knowing the Savior whom he loved and he vowed, if necessary, to die with Him. The moment he said, "I do not know [the Man]," Jesus "turned and looked at Peter. And Peter remembered the word of the Lord, how He had told him, 'Before a rooster crows today, you will deny Me three times.' And he went out and wept bitterly" (Luke 22:57–62). I wonder what it felt like to see the Lord's face after he denied knowing Him. Jesus knew Peter loved Him. Because He is omniscient, He knows the motives of our hearts too. One of the first things He did following His resurrection was to send a personal word to Peter that He had risen. That was a divine display of love for His suffering disciple (Mark 16:1, 4–7).

Even though he denied Him, Christ's love for Peter did not change. Jesus was God in the flesh. He doesn't change. If He did, He would no longer be God. He would be changeable, and He is not. He has chosen to love us with an eternal love, and nothing can alter this fact. He knew His disciple was struggling with deep regret and sorrow. Therefore, He sent a personal message of hope to Peter. It was as if Jesus was saying, "And be sure that you tell Peter to come too."

How many times have you felt that you have pushed the envelope too far in regard to disobedience? You may know that what you are doing is dead wrong, but you have given in to temptation and the desire to fulfill a sinful appetite. You wonder whether you have gone too far and whether God has stopped loving you. He hasn't, but He wants you to return to Him and give your heart back to Him in complete devotion.

Fear, thoughts of failure, and deep regret flooded Peter's mind, but Jesus' love for him had not been withdrawn. At the end of John's gospel we learn that the Savior not only restored his fellowship with him, but He also commissioned him for future service (John 21:15–17). God will never withdraw His love. He created you in love and He is committed to loving you no matter what. What changed Peter's life? Fear over being disciplined by God? No. It was love—the awesome, matchless, eternal, unconditional love of holy God who wants nothing more than for you and me to spend eternity with Him. This is His invitation to you: come and abide with Me in My love (John 15:9).

Nicodemus was a respected, prominent religious leader. He was a Pharisee and a member of the Sanhedrin. John recorded that he went to see Jesus at night—a time when he could be sure that no one would notice him with the Savior (John 3). Have you ever done a similar thing? Instead of professing your faith in God openly, you hang around in the background of conversations, hoping that you will go unnoticed. Jesus sees you. He knows you are there, and He knows if you are hiding rather than professing your trust in Him. The Lord understood the religious climate of His day, but when it came to loving Him and being one of His followers, there could be no half-hearted decisions. He knew the battle that was raging within Nicodemus's mind, but He did not make an exception. He demands our unbridled commitment, faith, and dedication. As I have said earlier: partial obedience is not obedience. We see this emerge in Nicodemus's life.

After the Crucifixion, Nicodemus helped another religious leader bury the Savior's body. The Bible tells us that he brought a hundred pounds of spices and ointments to place on the body of Jesus. He was definitely making a public confession. Burial spices were extremely expensive. People saved their entire lives in order to purchase them. Since he was a Pharisee and a member of the Sanhedrin, Nicodemus probably had the money needed to purchase these. Still his actions were a display of love and devotion for the Savior. He gave what he had reserved for his own burial. His decision was one of love and of passion for the Man he believed was the Messiah. His life was changed by God's love. It was not something he could explain. Until the Holy Spirit came, he probably did not fully understand the concept of John 3:16. Undoubtedly God's eternal love and forgiveness drew him to the Savior. He realized that the love of God was displayed on Calvary's cross, and it was the same love that beckoned him to draw near.

Zaccheus was a chief tax collector, despised by most people in his region. Usually the only friends of a man like him were people who had similar occupations. The fact was he did not just collect taxes; he was the head of the operation in his town or community. He was hated. Whenever people saw him coming, they wanted to avoid him. He would have been placed in the same social category as the prostitutes and others who were considered spiritually unclean. God's love for the sinner is amazing. He drew this man to Him. It is obvious that Zaccheus knew who Jesus was. The moment he heard that the Savior was headed his way, he dropped everything and went into the crowd, hoping to see Him. He was a very short man and finally had to climb a sycamore tree to get a glimpse of Jesus. Think about all the people who lined the street that day—each one wanted to touch or say something to the Lord. But Zaccheus caught Christ's attention. The Lord looked up into the tree and said, "Zaccheus, hurry and come down, for today I must stay at your house" (Luke 19:5). The Bible tells us that the people around them grumbled with envy and jealousy, "He has gone to be the guest of a man who is a sinner" (v. 7). Not only did Jesus stop to talk with him, but He told him, "I'm going home with you to eat dinner!"

Christ's response to Zaccheus was one of unconditional love. Even before they crossed the threshold of his home, the tax collector was seeking God's forgiveness and surrendering all that he had taken from the people: "Behold, Lord, half of my possessions I will give to the poor, and if I have defrauded anyone of anything, I will give back four times as much." Jesus said to him, "Today salvation has come to this house, because he, too, is a son of Abraham. For the Son of Man has come to seek and to save that which was lost" (vv. 8–10). When Jesus looked into the eyes of the publicly despised man, He saw someone who was emotionally and spiritually dead—a person who longed to know love and acceptance. And when Zaccheus looked into the eyes of Christ, he saw all that he longed to have and experience. He was accepted—not his sin—but who he was as a person. Immediately the wayward businessman came to a life-changing conclusion: he would rather have Jesus than any amount of gold and silver. God's love changes us. It is not demanding. However, the moment we get a taste of it, we want it all.

Before she met Jesus, the life of the *Samaritan woman* was full of personal tragedy, rejection, isolation, and unmentionable disappointment. She had been married several times, and the man she was living with was not her husband. The day the Savior found her, she was alone at the well drawing water. No respectable person wanted to be seen with her. We know this because women of honor did not come to draw water in the heat of the day. They usually went to the well with friends in the morning or later in the afternoon. Yet this woman had no one to befriend her. She came to the well alone and at a time of day when no one would hurl insults or demeaning remarks at her. Jesus did the unthinkable: He didn't just stop to talk with her; He asked her to draw Him a drink of water. Then what transpired in the aftermath of this request was nothing short of miraculous. He was a Jewish rabbi, someone who was supposed to view the people of Samaria as unclean. No respectable Jewish individual would travel through the area. Even though it was a shortcut to Galilee, the accepted route to take was around this region and not into it for fear of spiritual defilement. But a detail like this one has never prevented God from displaying His love for us. We are all sinners who are saved by His grace.

Jesus was alone with her. His disciples had gone to purchase something to eat. And the Lord made perfect use of the time they had to talk about her life and God's love: "If you knew the gift of God, and who it is who says to you, 'Give me a drink,' you would have asked Him, and He would have given you living water" (John 4:10). In those days, moving or flowing water was the best. He immediately grabbed her attention with these words. Then He told her, "Everyone who drinks of this [well] water will thirst again; but whoever drinks of the water that I will give him shall never thirst; but the water that I will give him will become in him a well of water springing up to eternal life" (vv. 13–14). Notice what God's love meant to her:

It offered eternal life.

It offered a way of forgiveness.

It was not judgmental.

It was living, and it was standing right in front of her.

Imagine how this woman felt. She had tried marriage once, and that did not work. She remarried a second, third, fourth, and fifth time, and each marriage ended in divorce. She must have felt totally rejected, like an outcast, as if no one cared. She had such a bad reputation that nobody would walk with her to draw water. But Jesus stopped to talk with her, and He told her all about the love of God. He did not condone her sin, but He viewed her through the eyes of love and told her how her life could change if she would believe in Him (John 4:15–29).

Many other examples appear in Scripture. The blind beggar named *Bartimaeus* (Mark 10:46) was considered an outcast. No one wanted to be with him. He was a blind man who had to beg for a living. And yet he called out to the Savior, "Jesus, Son of David, have mercy on me!" (v. 47). Some people might have stopped for him out of pity, but most walked quickly by him. The Son of God did not stop for a wealthy person, a religious leader, or a noted ruler; He stopped for a poor man who had been blind since birth.

God loves you and me just the way we are. Someone reading these words may say, "I feel as lonely and as forgotten as this man. I have no one. I'm not loved by anyone. I don't have friends. I go to work, and I come home at night. Some days, it is almost noon before anyone acknowledges that I'm alive and in the office. I just live from day to day—not going anywhere, not accomplishing anything. I'm a nobody." I want to reassure you that from God's perspective, you are somebody. He loves you and has a plan for your life. He healed Bartimaeus—a man who was blind, helpless, poor, and ragged. None of that mattered to Jesus. The focus of His heart was set on two things: salvation and restoration in this man's life.

You may be very sick and wonder what the future holds for you. Like Bartimaeus, you may feel as if you are no more than a poor beggar. The same Jesus who allowed you to be born and loved you even before you took your first breath has promised never to leave you. Nobody and nothing can make Him stop loving you. If you will turn to Him and take your eyes off yourself, you will discover that He has been beside you all this time, but you were spiritually blind to His presence.

This young man came to Jesus professing his love and desire to follow Him, but the Lord discerned the motivation of his heart (Mark 10:17–22). He knew that the man's wealth was more important to him than a personal relationship with Him. Jesus will never force Himself on us. His love is firm, but it also is gentle, understanding, and committed. He knows exactly where you are right now—in a home alone, an apartment with people living all around you, but no one to knock on your door. But if you will listen, you will hear Him knocking and calling to you.

The rich young ruler walked away because he knew he could not respond positively to what Jesus asked of him—an undivided heart. The Savior loved him (v. 21), but the young man loved his possessions more than he did God. Sometimes, I meet people who have accumulated a lot of wealth. After I listen to them for a while, I realize that although they have been amassing a fortune, their fortune has been accumulating them. They have become slaves to what they own. They have lost their freedom and are in bondage to their stocks, bonds, and the bank.

It does not matter how much money a person has; if he does not know the intimate and personal love of God, he is bankrupt. There is no peace, no sense of true joy, and no happiness for someone constantly threatened by the financial climate of the country. We need to invest wisely, but we invest our lives and our money so that we can give to others who have less.

God blesses us so we can be a blessing, not so we can horde what we have for personal satisfaction. The tragedy in this story is that Jesus knew this man's heart. He said, "Sell all that you own." In other words, "Don't have any other gods before Me." Jesus was not against wealth. But He is against it becoming a god in our lives.

This same principle applies to those with very little. I have talked with men and women who refuse to tithe. They want God to bless them, and they falsely believe that He does not love them because they have experienced one financial hardship after another. The tithe is important because it is an act of trust, love, and obedience. The widow who gave all that she had—two small copper coins—was far richer than the wealthiest person in the temple, because she gave out of her lack instead of out of her abundance (Mark 12:42). If you want to tell God that you really love Him, pray, but also give yourself to Him—every area—without reserve. Lay your life at His feet, and allow Him to raise you up at the proper time and teach you how to give and how to love correctly.

Each year during our missions conference at First Baptist Atlanta, I challenge our members to give sacrificially over and above their tithe to the work of missions through our church. A couple of years ago, a young man told me that he wanted to be a part of what God was doing, but he did not think he could give anything. Listening, I could tell that God was motivating him to give. I challenged him to take a step of faith and ask the Lord to show him what he should do. He replied, "Oh, I know the amount He wants me to give. I just don't think I can do it." I asked, "Do you trust Him to keep you safe when you lie down at night?" He answered yes and smiled. "Then you can trust Him with this." Giving to God, regardless of what we give, is a way for us to tell Him that we love Him, we trust Him, and we want to obey Him. He commands us to give (Luke 6:38). Not because He wants us to be poor, but for the opposite reason. He wants to bless us to an even greater degree, but He can't fill our hands if they are tightly closed around something that we believe has more value than God. This young man chose to trust God. He continued to tithe and also began to give each month to our missions program. At the end of a year, he came to see me, and his face was full of joy. He could barely contain himself as he told me all that God had done for him. God had blessed him in so many different ways.

Two things you need to remember: you cannot outgive God, and obedience always leads to blessings. If you obey Him, you may face difficulty because this is a part of life, but you will never go without having your needs met. He has promised, and He is faithful. In fact, He will fill your cup to the point where it overflows. What does giving have to do with love? Everything. Jesus gave Himself to us. His love is a free gift. He never stopped to think: *Giving My life as an atonement for their sins is just too much. I can't do that.* He gave freely because this is His way—giving and offering all that He has to you and me. There is no way we can repay the debt we owe Him. Either we accept His love, or we walk away like the rich young ruler. If we accept it, He will transform our lives the same way He transformed the lives of the woman caught in adultery (John 8:4) and the demon-possessed man (Mark 5:15).

Jesus even loved the man who betrayed Him, Judas. How do we know He loved him? Because God loves unconditionally. Judas wanted to manipulate Jesus into exercising His power as the Son of God. The disciple was a zealot, and he wanted Jesus to free Israel from Roman rule and domination. If he could get Jesus in the right situation, he thought the Savior would call down legions of angels to wipe out Israel's enemies. Then the kingdom of God would be established on earth, and Judas would be at the hub of the activity. He was wrong. Jesus came to seek those who were lost and to save them. He did not come to earth as a military ruler seeking to establish his kingdom. When Judas approached the Lord the night of His arrest, Jesus looked at him and called him "friend." God's unconditional love was paramount in Christ's life. It did not take long for Judas to realize what he had done and that he could never live with himself.

What kinds of people does Jesus love? All kinds. Do we ever betray Him? Yes, we do. Many times, we do this very thing with our silence and refusal to tell someone who is hurting and lost about the hope we have in Christ. The thief on the cross was aware of his sin (Luke 23:39–43). But he could not reconcile why Jesus had to suffer. Still, he believed in the Son of God, and that very day, he was with Jesus in paradise. No matter where you go, God loves you, and He is waiting for you to turn your life, your circumstances, and your future over to Him so He can bless you in awesome ways.

Chapter Eleven

GOD DELIGHTS
IN OBEDIENCE

Have you ever made a decision to obey God as a way of life? I'm not talking about obeying once in a while but in every area to the best of your knowledge and ability. Or do you find that there are times when you struggle to do what you know is right and in keeping with His principles? There may be times when it is easy to discern between what is right and in keeping with God's will and what is wrong and not a part of His plan. In fact, you may actually obey Him at crucial junctures because you want His best. Other times, you may feel as if you are being pulled aside by disobedience simply because you did not do your homework in prayer and the study of God's Word.

Solomon admonished us to "catch the foxes." He went on to explain that it is the "little foxes that are ruining the vineyards" (Song of Solomon 2:15). Often the smaller decisions bring about the biggest consequences. A decision to tell a little white lie is very costly because it leads to sin and usually the next step, which is deception. The enemy is very keen. He knows better than to tempt a seasoned believer to flat out disobey God. Obvious sin always draws a response. Friends and family members usually speak up when you are involved in something that leads to shame, failure, and a damaged testimony. You may falsely believe that something perceived as being insignificant is much easier to disguise. It may be for a season, but at some point God pulls the covers back, and the truth is revealed about what you have done.

Too many people reach the point of being shattered, broken, hurting, lonely, and discouraged before they seek God's help. A Christian counselor who works with corporate executives once told me that if he can be brought into a conflict before it escalates to a serious level, he usually can show people how to solve the problem. But this rarely happens because most of us are very reserved and will not freely expose what we are feeling and thinking until much later. By then the conflict is threatening to spiral out of control. Jesus knows our hearts, and He makes it clear from page one of His Word that obedience to Him should be our central focus. Adam and Eve disobeyed God and suffered the loss of everything they knew as right and good. However, just as you can track disobedience down through the generations, you also can trace the benefits of obedience. God provides a perfect contrast between the two in His Word:

> If you diligently obey the Lord your God, being careful to do all His commandments which I command you today, the Lord your God will set you high above all the nations of the earth. All these blessings will come upon you and overtake you if you obey the Lord your God: Blessed shall you be in the city, and blessed shall you be in the country. . . . But it shall come about, if you do not obey the Lord your God, to observe to do all His commandments and His statutes with which I charge you today, that all these curses will come upon you and overtake you: Cursed shall you be in the city, and cursed shall you be in the country. (Deut. 28:1–3, 15–16)

The only similarity between obedience and disobedience is that they reflect the type of lifestyle we have. If we have sincerely committed our lives to God, then we are going to obey Him; we are going to trust Him and leave all the consequences to Him. In times of disobedience, we lean on our own desires for direction. We vacillate back and forth between what we want to do and what we know is right.

What We Can Expect

God never intended for us to be harassed about the decisions we make each day. Sometimes when we pray, we immediately discern the will of God. Other times, we must wait, trusting Him to show us when and how to move forward. At still other times, He spends a great deal of time preparing us to step forward through an open door. But when the opportunity comes, we hesitate with feelings of worry and doubt. Then there are situations that result from a relaxed attitude about purity and holiness.

I cannot begin to count the number of times I asked a person why he or she allowed sin to gain such a stronghold. One man confessed that he had been around a certain type of sin most of his life. He did not have a clue about its influence on him until he realized that he did not have the joy and peace that he believed a Christian should experience. He had moments of happiness but nothing that lasted. He noticed that every time he tried to pray, his mind filled with images that were sinful and wrong. The enemy knows when we have withheld our obedience to God. Like a well-trained warrior, he moves in for the attack, but often his approach is not a full frontal assault. It is subtle and hidden, like a landmine just below the surface. The mistake we make is in assuming that we can ignore God's commandment to obey Him and not suffer harm.

The bottom line is that there is never a time when it is okay to disobey God. We should obey Him regardless of what we think or how we feel. It is a matter of choice, but one that many Christians do not yet understand or submit to. Far too often, people evaluate their circumstances according to what they perceive will profit them: *How will this help me get ahead?* or *Will this move be beneficial to my future?* We say we believe God is all-wise and knows what is best for us, but often we end up looking for advice from people around us and not from the only One who knows everything we need to know. We need to consider only one issue: *Is this God's will for my life?*

Disobedience is not always wrapped in a sinful-looking package. Yes, it is sinful to disobey God because it hurts the heart of Someone who has a plan for our lives. It damages our fellowship with Him and leads to feelings of guilt and shame. But far too often when we hear the word *disobedience*, we think of a sexual sin or some habit that is just dead wrong. However, we disobey God when we refuse to do what He has gifted, trained, and called us to do. Our refusal to be open to His plan can bring misery and regret. On our own, we do not have significant insight into the future. All we can do is make choices based on what may or may not take place. When all is said and done, only one Person has absolute knowledge, and that is the Lord. And He has promised to provide the guidance that we need:

> Trust in the LORD with all your heart
> And do not lean on your own understanding.
> In all your ways acknowledge Him,
> And He will make your paths straight.
> Do not be wise in your own eyes;
> Fear the LORD and turn away from evil.
> It will be healing to your body
> And refreshment to your bones. (Prov. 3:5–8)

We can worry, fret, and fume about an issue that God has already dealt with and has moved on to another point. But if we trust Him, we will obey Him each and every time. Being obedient does not mean that we will never face difficult decisions. It means that when we do, we will resolve that He has gone before us, and because we have committed our lives to Him, the way we travel will be straight, sure, and manageable. The prophet Isaiah reassured us,

> The LORD will continually guide you,
> And satisfy your desire in scorched places,
> And give strength to your bones;
> And you will be like a watered garden,
> And like a spring of water whose waters do not fail. (58:11)

Notice that both passages of Scripture speak of physical health and well-being. That is what obedience does for us. It disposes of the raw emotions that tie us up in knots inside.

You may be living in complete obedience, and yet you are battling a serious illness. Your situation does not mean you have done something wrong. On the other hand, if you believe in God but refuse to trust Him completely or to obey Him, then you are going to feel stressed, pressured, out of control, and fearful. Disobedience can be as simple as not trusting Him to take care of your immediate need at home, in your community, or on your job.

On many occasions I have talked with educators who confess to feeling utterly burned out. They have short emotional fuses and are tired. When I ask them if they have shared all of this with the Lord in prayer, many look surprised and comment that they felt He was already aware of their needs. Part of the obedience process is learning to open your hands to Him and give Him your deepest cries of frustration. Healing cannot take place when you are holding on to hurt or frustration. Lay it on His altar and allow Him to restore you. There are many facets surrounding obedience but only one way to accomplish it, and that is through surrender to the One who loves you and has a plan for your life and circumstances.

Friends are God-given resources, but they may provide unwise counsel and wrong information. The very thing they feel is the best for your life may not be what God wants you to do. Therefore, it is always best to listen to their counsel, especially when they are committed believers, but also to pray and ask the Lord to make His will absolutely clear so you will not take a wrong turn—mentally, emotionally, spiritually, or physically. You can avoid a lot of heartache by obeying God.

Obedience Is a Choice

I doubt that many of us would consider some of the minor decisions we make each day and wonder whether they contain some hint or clue to the future. Often we make choices based on what we think or feel is right. The interest rates are low; therefore, it must be the right time to purchase a house. We have driven our car for almost ten years; it is time to get another one. We have just had our second child; therefore, we need another bedroom plus a home office. We have worked at the same business for years, and the new CEO is not very understanding; it must be time to move on to the next place. Some of these statements are reasonable, but only if the outcome or the choice is one that God initiates.

Peter was faced with a life-changing decision (Luke 5). The outcome of his choice would determine his future. Jesus had been preaching along the shore of the lake of Gennesaret (the Sea of Galilee). I imagine the crowd was quite large. His ministry was growing; word had spread about how He had healed those who were sick with various diseases (Luke 4:40). By the time Luke reached chapter 5 in his account of Christ's earthly ministry, it was obvious that the people were hungry to hear Jesus preach and to be near Him. On several occasions, I have spoken to large groups of people and watched as they began to move forward. The people in the back leaned in to hear, and in doing so, they pushed against the ones in the front. With His back to the water and the people "pressing" on Him, Jesus had no place to go (Luke 5:1).

Peter the fisherman was also there, listening to some degree as he mended his nets in preparation for going back out on the lake later that evening. It was an odd request, but when Jesus asked the fisherman to allow Him to enter the boat and then to move it off shore a short distance, he agreed. That was Peter's first step toward obedience.

The point that I want to make here is that obedience is a process. It is not a gift. Salvation is a gift. God's grace demonstrated toward us is a gift He gives each one of us when we accept Him as our Savior. This amazing gift of unconditional love is not something we can work to achieve. Obedience is different, however. God doesn't necessarily want us to work to achieve it; He wants it to be our first nature. We obey Him because of who He is. In the last chapter I mentioned that partial obedience is not obedience. After all, how can we halfway obey God?

Either Peter did what Jesus requested, or he said no. Here Peter said yes, but notice what else he said: "[Jesus] got into one of the boats, which was Simon's, and asked him to put out a little way from the land. And He sat down and began teaching the people from the boat. When He had finished speaking, He said to Simon, 'Put out into the deep water and let down your nets for a catch.' Simon answered and said, 'Master, we worked hard all night and caught nothing, but I will do as You say and let down the nets'" (Luke 5:3–5). In these verses, we are given an outline of obedience. Many times, the ways of God include specific steps, and we find some in Luke 5.

Step One: Peter was nearby listening to Jesus. The Lord knew that he was there and that he had an empty boat.

Step Two: Jesus entered Peter's boat so He would be able to address the crowd better.

Step Three: Peter listened to Jesus' request. He responded by explaining that he was completely unsuccessful the night before in his attempt to catch fish. Nevertheless, he obeyed the Lord, raised the sails on his ship, and headed out into deep water.

Step Four: Peter received the reward of his obedience.

What would have happened if Peter had said, "No, I spent the entire night out on that water, and if there had been any fish available, I would have caught them"? We can't dismiss the fact that he was a seasoned fisherman. He knew the waters like we know the backs of our hands. He grew up by the lake, and he understood the components of a productive fishing business—or at least he thought he did.

Here is what God did so that we know He meant business and was involved. The night before, Peter caught nothing—not one single fish. He came in the next morning, having been up all night pulling and dragging nets around a small, uncomfortable boat. All he wanted to do was clean his nets and go home to take a short nap so he would have the energy to get up and go back out that evening. But Jesus showed up with a crowd of people, and the next thing Peter knew, his boat had become the Savior's stage. That was okay. He could say, "Yes, You can use my boat while I finish doing what I am doing." It was not a difficult decision, but he had to agree to it. Step One was accomplished.

The next step was more difficult: not only was he tired, but his friends were close by, watching to see what he would do. When Jesus told Peter to head out into deep water where he would catch a large draw of fish, they probably rolled their eyes. A young Rabbi, whom they were sure knew nothing about fishing, was telling Peter—the master, the ace, the CEO of the shoreline—what to do.

Can't you imagine John and James looking at each other and thinking, *Oh, no, what is Peter going to say?* What would you have said? You probably know the ending to the story so you might be inclined to say, "I would have raised the sails and headed out into the deep." But would you? Have you, when He has called to you asking that you would obey Him? Obedience looks different when He is asking us to do something that personally costs us more than we think we can afford. Scripture doesn't tell us whether

Peter scanned the scene or looked to his buddies for help. It just tells us one thing: he obeyed the Lord and stated, "Master, . . . I will do as You say and let down the nets."

I can imagine that silence fell on those who were on the shore as they watched Peter release the anchor, raise his sails, and turn his rudder toward deep water. You may ask, "What motivated him to do this? Is it something that I can experience in my life?" I believe it is, but you must trust God—not pull out your calculator and add up all that you could gain and all that you could lose. This faith comes by hearing God's voice and responding in pure obedience.

People have told me, "I just don't know whether God wants me to do this. It doesn't make sense." Going back out to fish during the heat of the morning did not make sense to Peter. No one went fishing then. It was hot, and the fish went to the bottom of the lake—a place where nets could not reach. At night, they were closer to the surface of the water. My obedience today prepares me for my obedience tomorrow, and tomorrow's prepares me for the next day and for the years to come. The fish were not available the night before, but the next day, in the heat of the morning, they were right where God wanted them to be. There are no coincidences with God. Nothing "just" happens. He always has a plan, and that plan reflects His ways. If you want to walk in step with Him, then you will learn how to be obedient. Luke told us that once the nets were down, they began to fill with fish to a point of breaking. Do you realize the miracle that took place? There were no fish the night before, but at a time when none should be present, the waters were teeming. There were so many that Peter had to signal for John and the others to join him. His boat was about to sink, and he did not know what he would do. All he could utter were these words to the Savior: "Go away from me Lord, for I am a sinful man" (Luke 5:8).

"Amazement had seized him and all his companions because of the catch of fish which they had taken" (v. 9). Not only was Peter at the hub of this miracle, but others drew near also. Many times when we are obedient, those around us join in the blessing. I'm convinced that none of these men had ever seen so many fish in their nets at one time. The nets were bursting, the boats were about to sink, and Peter fell down on his knees and worshiped the Lord. Here is one truth on which you can stake your life: if Jesus asks you to do something, you know without a doubt that a blessing will follow. Questioning, doubting, calculating—none of these build the faith that He wants you to have and exhibit. This does not mean that you will never make a mistake. It means that the motivation of your heart, to the best of your ability, is set on obeying God. Remember Abraham left his home at God's instruction, not knowing where the Lord would lead. Moses went back to Egypt without knowing all that his new role as deliverer would involve. Esther approached the king, not knowing if she would lose her life. Rahab hid the spies who came to view the promised land. Mary heard the angel's voice and said, "Behold, the [handmaid] of the Lord" (Luke 1:38). And Peter said, "I will do as You say and let down the nets" (Luke 5:5). The Christian life requires obedience.

You and I learn obedience. We are not born with the desire to obey God or anyone in authority. It is a learning process. When you were born, you grew to a certain age, and then you began to test how far you could go before your dad or mom gave you a warning. At first, you may have listened when your parents said no, and you stopped what you were doing. But there quickly came a point—even before your first birthday—when you decided that ignoring the word *no* was not a big deal. But it became a big deal when you continued to ignore their warning and rebuke. If you do not like authority, then you are going to rebel against it. Often children grow up naturally rebelling because their parents do not teach them to obey. If there is a spirit of obedience ruling your life, then you are going to willingly and lovingly choose to be obedient. There are certain rules that we have to obey. Peter did not instantly know to obey Jesus. He did know there was something in

Christ's life, and that something drew him near enough for him to know that this Man was not a typical teacher. Then when his nets filled to overflowing with fish, he dropped to his knees and proclaimed, "Lord!"

Here is one of Satan's traps: God places an opportunity before you, and suddenly you wonder whether He opened the door. You analyze the situation from a human perspective: "If this happens, then I know God is involved. If I get this piece of information, it is His will and I will go forward." That is not obedience. If Peter had taken time to go through a mental Rolodex of information about Jesus, he might never have pushed away from the shore. The Holy Spirit was the One who brought Peter to the point of obedience. Earlier we talked about how we come to know Jesus as Savior. His Spirit must draw us, and that was exactly what happened with Peter. He knew that the Man who was in his boat was much more than an everyday teacher. He was from God.

Another way Satan can trip us is by telling us that God leaves some issues up to us. He whispers, "This is not a big deal. It doesn't matter what you decide at this juncture. If it was something really huge, then God would let you know what you should do." As hard as it is to believe, young people—who have married and then realized they had many differences—have come to me and said that they did not realize God had a plan in this area. Some are believers, but they never really took a serious amount of time to pray and ask God to give them the right marriage partner. Others may have married unbelievers, and their lives are miserable because suddenly they are unequally yoked (2 Cor. 6:14). We could list many, many situations where we have jumped into a situation without asking God what is best. Nothing is insignificant to God. Peter's journey into obedience began with a simple action. Jesus got in his boat and began teaching God's truth. Don't be tempted to think that Peter did not have a choice. He could have asked Jesus to leave, but he didn't and his life was totally changed in a matter of moments.

God wants to fill your life with good things. He has so many rewards, but for the most part, they are not like the rewards of this world. You may achieve a certain level of success, but it will fade. You can earn large sums of money, but not a dime will go with you to heaven. Only God's rewards are eternal. Only His blessings bring the peace and joy you long to have. The way He operated in Peter's life is the same way He will operate in your life. You may not be standing on a shoreline cleaning a bunch of nets, but without a doubt there will be a time when He will come to you and say, "Move your boat out into deep water, and let down your nets for a catch."

Not only did Peter have to move his boat away from shore, but he had to gather up all his nets—make sure they were folded and ready to go—and then he had to raise his sails so he could go back out on the water. He left the shoreline wondering what would happen next. And when something marvelous happened, he was ready to change occupations. The issue is: what is God's will for your life? Peter realized what His will was for him, but you must come to a point where you know that you are living the life He has planned for you to live. Once He has made this clear and after you have made the decision to obey Him, the feelings of worry stop, the fretting ends, and the chatter of "what if" fades. You may face feelings of doubt again, however. And if you do, you may have to go back to God and ask Him to encourage your heart and help you recall the verses He gave you that brought finalization, hope, and clarity.

How would you categorize your life? Would you say that you are committed to obeying the Lord, but you want to make sure that what you do will be best for you? Or would you say, "I just have this feeling inside every time someone tells me what to do. A wave comes over me, and I can sense this feeling building within that makes me want to say, 'I know what I'm doing, and I know what is best'"? Someone reading this may think, *My father was so demanding that I just want to say no to authority no matter what is involved.* These are harsh statements, but I have heard ones like them and more.

The truth is: if you do not come to a conclusion of faith and obedience—it takes both—then your life is going to be outlined by defeat, failure, disappointment, suffering, and one wrong decision after another. You must believe in the One God has sent to you. The outcome of Peter's faith was a new line of work—one that had an eternal purpose. Jesus said to him, "Do not fear, from now on you will be catching men" (Luke 5:10). What an awesome way to live the rest of your life—in the shadow of His constant care, in the light of His truth and eternal glory!

Chapter Twelve

IN STEP WITH GOD'S PLAN

A few years ago, I was in Nova Scotia on vacation and to do some photography. As I was walking along the beach, I came upon a small, deserted boat. Its owner had pulled it to shore, placed the oars inside, and left it. It was just a rowboat, but immediately I sensed the Lord saying, *They left everything.* A wave of emotion swept over me because I knew He was reminding me of Peter, James, and John and the day they pulled their boats to shore and left them. It was their last official day of work as earthly fishermen. Luke wrote, "When they had brought their boats to land, they left everything and followed Him" (Luke 5:11). Instead of basking in their newly found fame, the men made a life-changing decision: they would follow the Savior. Things that had seemed so right and familiar hours earlier were no longer important or valuable to them. Their goals, dreams, and desires had changed that quickly. Peter's businessman veneer fell away, and his love for holy God was revealed.

How do you walk in step with God? You make yourself available for a personal, loving, intimate relationship with Jesus Christ. How can you know His ways and plans for your life? You draw near to Him with an open heart and a desire to obey only Him.

Walking in Step with God

Every once in a while, someone will come up to me at the end of a service and say that God is calling him or her into Christian work, but the person is reluctant to proceed because of a lack of education. Jesus was the One who trained Peter and the others for service. No one in that early group of disciples had a degree in Bible and theology or any other related area. But they did have a hunger for God and a desire to know and serve Him. *The first step to walking with God is availability. The second is desire.* I'm not saying that going to seminary or Bible college is unnecessary; education is very important. I am saying that God knew how He was going to use Peter, James, and John, and He wanted to teach them about Himself from personal experience.

If your desire is to please the Lord, He will make sure you are in the center of His will. But far too often, we make decisions based on whether we think we will be successful or not. Peter did not do this. He did not look at the fish that were filling his boat and think, *This Man is going places. I want to be a part of His team.* He just knew that there was something irresistible about being with Jesus. He realized He was from God, and Peter wanted to know Him—His ways and methods. You will never be able to figure out all the ways that God works in your life and in the world around you. But as it was with Peter and the others, there will come a point where you fall to your knees and proclaim your faith and trust in Him.

The third step to walking with God is obedience, which we addressed in the previous chapter. Everything in Peter's fishing business changed on one trip. Remember that they were fishing at the wrong time of day, and they were in the wrong place—deep water. Have you ever been tempted to think, *I can't do this. I have no idea where this will lead?* If you have, more than likely God has led you into deep water where He can work a mighty miracle. Can you imagine Peter hearing the Savior's command to sail out into water that was far too deep to go fishing? He probably thought, *There is no way this is going to happen.* But it did, and it will for you too. Peter recognized Jesus' authority, and he obeyed. There will come a time when God will require you to do the same—launch out and leave your comfort zone for a place where you must trust Him and not your ability to get the job done. You won't be able to touch the bottom of the lake or the pool. No human line of security will be available. There will be only one line of hope, and that is the one tied to Him—and it is all you need.

When my son, Andy, was young, he became very interested in obeying God. He wanted to know what would happen if the Lord told him to do something and he failed to do it. Would he have a second, third, or fourth opportunity? I reassured him that obedience and faith are steps in the process of knowing God.

How do we learn about the ways of God? We gain experience by being with Him through prayer and the study of His Word. Sometimes, it may mean just taking time to be still in His presence and not feel that we have to do anything but be with Him. We are not going to get everything right all the time. We will make mistakes—both large and small.

Over the course of his life, Peter made several mistakes that are recorded in the New Testament. We discussed these in chapter 10. He failed to see the eternal plan of God when Jesus told him and the others that He would die. But Jesus never withheld His love from His disciple. On a stormy sea, Peter began walking to the Lord, only to be distracted by the wind and the waves. He immediately began to sink, and he cried out for the Lord to save him. And the Savior reached down and pulled him up. One of his gravest mistakes was his denial on the very night when Jesus needed him the most. But after His resurrection, Jesus forgave, restored, and commissioned Peter for service in His kingdom work on earth.

He knows there will be times when you will fail miserably and He will have to lift you up. He is your Savior, and He sees the future and the times that you will obey, follow, and do all that He has planned for you to do. You have hope at every turn because no matter how the road divides, He is there to meet and walk with you.

There was another mistake in Peter's life that we did not note earlier. Peter witnessed firsthand the early years of ministry that God had given Paul, the Apostle to the Gentiles. He even ate what the new Gentile believers were eating. They had received the Holy Spirit and were baptized. Peter was elated. But later in Jerusalem when he was back in the company of his peers, he resumed his strictly Jewish lifestyle—saying that the Gentiles must be circumcised and adhere to traditions of the church in Jerusalem. When Paul visited Jerusalem, he confronted Peter, reminding him how God had worked in the lives of the Gentile community and how he had joined in their celebration over their salvation.

The underlying problem was that Peter was not relying on God's Spirit. He was worried about what others would think if they found out that he had put his full stamp of approval on the new Christians who were living by faith in the Son of God. God's ways are higher than our ways. His thoughts are higher than our thoughts. The ways of God involve the Crucifixion, the resurrection, and the outpouring of the Holy Spirit in the lives of men and women who long to know and serve Him. Peter learned an awesome lesson. Many times what we think is right is not what God says should happen. If we refuse to drop our guards and follow Him, we will miss His ways.

Another failure for Peter occurred during the Last Supper that he shared with Jesus. I mention it last because it is essential to knowing God. Most of us recall that when the disciples were gathered in the Upper Room, Jesus took a towel and a basin of water and began washing the feet of each man. The person who was the lowest servant usually performed this task. But the disciples looked up, and Jesus was tying a towel around His waist. He was going to wash their feet.

Humility is crucial to our relationship with God. You can be the brightest and smartest individual, but if you are not humble in heart and spirit, God cannot use you. Jesus was humble in spirit, but His disciples needed to learn what it meant to serve others in this way. They would not be the ones out front receiving the praise of the people. If that was their goal, they could not serve Him. Their only goal was to do the will of the One who sent them. Nothing else could be placed before this.

Each disciple submitted to Christ's care. They allowed the Savior to wash their feet, but when He approached Peter, He received a different response. Peter recoiled and said, "'Never shall You wash my feet!' Jesus answered him, 'If I do not wash you, you have no part with Me'" (John 13:8). Don't ever boast about how strong or smart you are. Don't elaborate about what you will do and what you won't do. That is pride, and it blocks the Lord from teaching you the best way to live the Christian life. Peter realized that Jesus' actions were a display of humility. It was humiliating for him to sit down and watch the Son of God, the Messiah, the Christ, the Lord of lords, the King of kings wash his feet. What was the lesson God wanted him and the others to learn? It was that humility comes before service. Without this, we cannot serve Him. We can work hard—to the point of burnout—but we can't serve with love and a desire to understand what He wants to teach us.

Some people find this a very difficult lesson to learn, but if we are committed to knowing God in a personal and intimate way, we will be just as committed to allowing Him to humble us so that we can be molded and shaped for His glory. What has more value than this? Nothing. If you had the opportunity (and you do) to live for holy God, knowing that He will bless you in ways you cannot imagine, or to live for yourself, what would you do? Would you continue to struggle to get ahead, to push to the front of some imaginary pack of people going somewhere that leads only to earthly reward? I doubt very seriously that if we could see beyond this moment to the plans that God has for us, we would choose the second choice. No one in his or her right mind would ignore the gift of God that has been given to each one of us through His Son.

Yet many people have been spiritually blinded by their desires and false beliefs. And I'm not saying that we should quit our jobs and take off in different directions. I'm saying that when our lives are focused on Jesus Christ, we will be successful with all we do. There is a difference between serving Him and others and serving only ourselves. When we serve God, we receive eternal rewards and benefits—some of which we will not experience until we are with Him in heaven. Service only to ourselves often ends in disappointment and sorrow.

The fourth step is answering His call. Peter had two options: he could go with Jesus, or he could continue the life he had been living. Each one of these steps requires faith, but this one reveals more about us than any of the others. It is easy to say, "But what if this is not what God is saying? What do I do then?" or "What if I make a mistake? I can't go back?" First of all, if you are truly listening for God's voice, you will know what He wants you to do. Jesus said, "Do not fear, from now on you will be catching men" (Luke 5:10). Even if you discern some of God's methods, you will not have absolute knowledge about every detail. Only He has that.

God knew the plan, and the question before these men was simply this: "Will you follow Me?" Everything boils down to your relationship with Jesus Christ. Peter and the others instantly felt a connection with the Savior. They realized nothing from that point on would be the same, and they were right. God changed the direction of their lives and placed them on a course of eternal blessing. Before the Lord could do that, however, each man had to answer the call.

One of the saddest moments comes when someone tells me that he sensed God urging him to go in a certain direction, but he failed to do it. He never followed the Lord. He continued to go to church and even volunteered, but he never made a full commitment to do whatever God asked him to do. Not everyone will be in the ministry. But there are countless ways He can use us. If we refuse, we will never know the extent of our full potential. Anytime we find ourselves arguing or negotiating with God about why we cannot do what He has given us to do, we are headed for trouble.

If you feel that you have said no to God, then I want to assure you that you can begin again. You can tell Him that you are sorry that you made the wrong decision and chose not to listen to or obey His call. You and I must come to a point in our lives where we say, "From this point on, I'm going to be obedient to God and do whatever He asks me to do. I want this to be reflective of my lifestyle. I want to surrender so that I can know Him and understand why He does what He does." But if you keep fighting the same old battles with the same fleshly desires, you are going to struggle.

Another thing you must remember is that knowing God and learning His ways involve a lifelong process. Even after spending three years with Jesus, Peter still did not understand what was going on the night that the Savior was arrested. In fact, he was the one in the garden who came to the Lord's defense and cut off the ear of a Roman soldier. He had not grasped the fact that Jesus' arrest was a part of God's plan. He could not see beyond the horror of that one moment. But after the resurrection and the coming of the Holy Spirit, his spiritual eyesight became 20/20. Even then, he continued to learn through his victories and mistakes. Each time he got it right, he learned something else about God. And each time he failed, he learned about God's mercy, grace, love, and plan for him. Peter would not advise us to follow in his footsteps. Sin is costly. But as he discovered, the well of God's grace is an infinite source of forgiveness.

A Heart That Is Set on Obedience

When your heart is fully committed to the Lord, you will grow in your faith and have discerning insight into the world around you. Your knowledge will not be limited to what you feel. Feelings have nothing to do with the Christian life. They change. One moment you may "feel" close to God, and the next hour or so you don't. You think, *What has happened? Has He left me?* No. He never changes, He never leaves, and He never abandons you. One of the enemy's favorite methods of operation is to tempt us into feeling a certain way that is nowhere near reality. What is true? The unconditional love of God. What is unshakable? The love of God. What is the one thing that will never change? His love for you and me.

At the end of a morning service during our time of invitation, a young man walked down the aisle and came up to me. He said, "Pastor, I woke up this morning, and I turned on the television and saw your program. I was just flipping channels and stopped to see what you were saying. I don't go to church, but it was as if something or someone was urging me to get up, get dressed, and go. I don't know how I knew this, but God spoke to my heart as I was lying in my bed watching TV. He said, *Get up and drive to First Baptist and give your life to Me this morning.* And this is what I want to do."

Suppose he had responded, "Go to church? I haven't been in a long time. I will have to get up, take a shower, shave, get dressed, and by that time it will be late. So, why don't I just continue to lie here?" How many times has God spoken to you, and you have given Him an excuse? This young man obeyed God because God had something in mind for his life. When He speaks to a lost person so strongly, directly, clearly with great authority, He has something in mind. And if you are a believer and you have given God one excuse after another, then you are missing the wondrous gifts and blessings that He has for you. He will not force you to know Him.

Though you may not realize it, we have talked about choice throughout this entire book. God made a choice to love you and me with an unconditional love. Through grace, He chose to save you and offer you the gift of eternal life. Now, the choice is yours to make. This young man did not realize it, but when he decided to obey God, he positioned himself for great blessing—not the blessings of this world but the blessings of God, which are infinite in number and eternal in value. Every time we humble ourselves before Him, He reveals a little more about Himself to us. A lot of things in this life may seem attractive, but nothing you will ever experience will satisfy your heart and soul like Jesus Christ.

Can you understand the ways of God? Absolutely. Can you know the plans He has for your life? Yes, you can, but you must make a decision to seek Him. When you do, you will find Him, and you also will discover all you could ever hope to know and have. The pattern of your life will fall right in step with God's plan and will. And as a result, the joy you will experience will be unending and without measure. This is His promise: seek Me with a whole heart and you will find Me (Matt. 7:7).

About the Author

Dr. Charles F. Stanley is pastor of the 16,000-member First Baptist Church in Atlanta, Georgia, and is head of the international In Touch® Ministries. He has twice been elected president of the Southern Baptist Convention and is known internationally from his radio and television program *In Touch*. His many best-selling books include *When the Enemy Strikes*, *Finding Peace*, *Landmines in the Path of the Believer*, *Enter His Gates*, *The Source of My Strength*, and *How to Listen to God*.

OTHER BOOKS BY CHARLES STANLEY

Charles Stanley's
Handbook for Christian Living

Discover Your Destiny

Eternal Security

Finding Peace

The Gift of Forgiveness

How to Handle Adversity

How to Keep Your Kids on Your Team

How to Listen to God

Into His Presence

Our Unmet Needs

On Holy Ground

Seeking His Face

The Source of My Strength

Success God's Way When the Enemy Strikes

Winning the War Within

The Wonderful Spirit-Filled Life

Landmines in the Path of the Believer

10 Principles for Studying Your Bible

When Your Children Hurt

Stuck in Reverse

Living in the Power of the Holy Spirit

Finding Peace

Pathways to His Presence

Walking Wisely

THE LIFE PRINCIPLES SERIES

Advancing Through Adversity
Study Guide

Becoming Emotionally Whole
Study Guide

Developing a Servant's Heart
Study Guide

Developing Inner Strength
Study Guide

Discovering Your Identity in Christ
Study Guide

Experiencing Forgiveness
Study Guide

Leaving a Godly Legacy
Study Guide

Protecting Your Family
Study Guide

Relying on the Holy Spirit
Study Guide

Sharing the Gift of Encouragement
Study Guide

Talking with God
Study Guide

Understanding Eternal Security
Study Guide

Understanding Financial Stewardship
Study Guide

Winning on the Inside
Study Guide

The Charles F. Stanley Life Principles Bible
(NKJV)

The Charles F. Stanley Life Principles Bible
(NASB)

The Charles F. Stanley Life Principles Daily
Bible

Do you ever wish you could have more of In Touch at your fingertips?

Dr. Stanley and In Touch Ministries are just a click away. Find exactly what you need faster and easier than ever before at *InTouch.org*.

Log on now to:

- Watch and listen to Dr. Stanley's messages.
- Read daily devotions and inspiring articles from *In Touch* magazine.
- Get answers to your questions about God.
- Download In Touch Podcasts.
- Support In Touch by donating online.
- Discover how to have a life full of joy and purpose.
- Shop at the easy-to-use online bookstore.
- Find strength to help you through difficult times.
- See how In Touch is reaching people around the world.
- Learn how you can make a difference in your own home and community.
- Enjoy special online offers.

In Touch's mission is to lead people worldwide into a growing relationship with Jesus Christ and to strengthen the local church. Whether you're a new believer or a mature Christian, InTouch.org can help you draw closer to God. Log on to *InTouch.org* today and take advantage of all the great things In Touch Ministries has to offer.

Go to www.InTouch.org
for a FREE
subscription or call
Customer Care at
1-800-789-1473

AVAILABLE
NOW

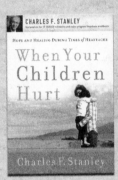

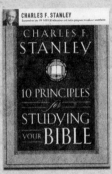

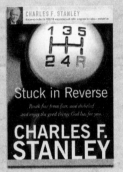

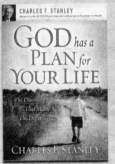

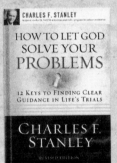

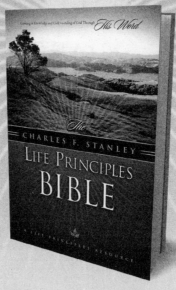

The CHARLES F. STANLEY LIFE PRINCIPLES BIBLE delivers Stanley's cherished values to benefit every Christian in their life's pursuits. With almost 200,000 in print, The *Charles F. Stanley Life Principles Bible* communicates the life principles Dr. Stanley has gleaned from the Word through his years of Bible teaching and pastoral ministry. The result is a Bible overflowing with practical articles, notes, and sidebars that help readers understand what the Bible has to say about life's most important questions.

Features include:

- 30 Life Principles, with articles throughout the Bible
- Life Lessons
- Life Examples from the people of the Bible
- "Answers to Life's Questions" articles
- God's Promises for Life index to get into the Scripture Book Introductions
- "What the Bible Says About" articles
- Concordance
- Available in both the New King James Version and New American Standard Bible